MASTERING MACHINE LEARNING: ALGORITHMS CONCEPTS AND TECHNIQUES

S.GEERTHIK

L. HARI PRASATH

L. ALPHIN EZHIL MANUEL

G.SINDHU

ANISH.T.P

MASTERING THE CORPORATE MAZE

A GUIDE FOR ORGANISATIONAL SURVIVAL

MANOJ N G

notionpress.com

INDIA • SINGAPORE • MALAYSIA

ISBN
Paperback 979-8-89632-842-1
Hardcase 979-8-89777-338-1

Contents

Contents

## CHAPTER ONE

Introduction

Machine Learning (ML) is a subset of artificial intelligence (AI) that focuses on building systems capable of learning from data, identifying patterns, and making decisions with minimal human intervention. Instead of being explicitly programmed, ML algorithms use statistical techniques to improve their performance over time as they are exposed to more data.

Key Concepts in Machine Learning

1. **Data:**

   - Data is the foundation of ML. It can be structured (e.g., tables, databases) or unstructured (e.g., images, text, audio).
   - The quality and quantity of data directly impact the performance of ML models.

2. **Features:**

   - Features are the input variables used to make predictions.
   - Feature engineering involves selecting, transforming, and creating meaningful features from raw data.

3. **Model:**

   - A model is a mathematical representation of a real-world process. It learns patterns from data to make predictions or decisions.
   - Examples: Linear regression, decision trees, neural networks.

4. **Training:**

- Training is the process of teaching a model to learn patterns from data by adjusting its parameters.
- The model is trained on a labeled dataset (supervised learning) or an unlabeled dataset (unsupervised learning).

5. **Evaluation:**

- After training, the model is evaluated on unseen data to measure its performance.
- Common evaluation metrics include accuracy, precision, recall, F1-score, and mean squared error (MSE).

6. **Inference:**

- Once trained, the model is used to make predictions on new, unseen data.

Types of Machine Learning

1. **Supervised Learning:**

- The model learns from labeled data, where the input features are paired with the correct output (target variable).
- Examples: Classification (e.g., spam detection) and regression (e.g., predicting house prices).
- Algorithms: Linear regression, logistic regression, support vector machines (SVM), random forests.

2. **Unsupervised Learning:**

- The model learns from unlabeled data, identifying patterns or structures without explicit guidance.
- Examples: Clustering (e.g., customer segmentation) and dimensionality reduction (e.g., PCA).
- Algorithms: K-means clustering, hierarchical clustering, DBSCAN, t-SNE.

3. **Semi-Supervised Learning:**

- ◦ Combines labeled and unlabeled data to improve learning accuracy.
- ◦ Useful when labeled data is scarce or expensive to obtain.

4. **Reinforcement Learning:**

- ◦ The model learns by interacting with an environment and receiving feedback in the form of rewards or penalties.
- ◦ Examples: Game playing (e.g., AlphaGo), robotics, self-driving cars.
- ◦ Algorithms: Q-learning, deep Q-networks (DQN), policy gradients.

Steps in a Machine Learning Workflow

1. **Problem Definition:**

- ◦ Define the problem and determine if ML is the right solution.
- ◦ Identify the goal (e.g., prediction, classification, clustering).

2. **Data Collection:**

- ◦ Gather data from various sources (e.g., databases, APIs, sensors).
- ◦ Ensure the data is relevant and representative of the problem.

3. **Data Cleaning and Preprocessing:**

- ◦ Handle missing values, outliers, and inconsistencies.
- ◦ Normalize, scale, and encode data for ML algorithms.

4. **Feature Engineering:**

- ◦ Select, transform, and create features to improve model performance.

5. **Model Selection:**

- ◦ Choose an appropriate algorithm based on the problem type (e.g., regression, classification).

6. **Model Training:**

- Train the model on the training dataset.
- Use techniques like cross-validation to avoid overfitting.

7. **Model Evaluation:**

- Evaluate the model on a test dataset using relevant metrics.
- Iterate and improve the model if necessary.

8. **Model Deployment:**

- Deploy the trained model to a production environment for real-world use.
- Monitor and update the model as needed.

9. **Model Maintenance:**

- Continuously monitor the model's performance and retrain it with new data if necessary.

Applications of Machine Learning

1. **Healthcare:**

- Disease prediction, medical imaging analysis, drug discovery.

2. **Finance:**

- Fraud detection, credit scoring, algorithmic trading.

3. **Retail:**

- Recommendation systems, demand forecasting, inventory management.

4. **Natural Language Processing (NLP):**

- Sentiment analysis, chatbots, language translation.

5. **Computer Vision:**

   - Facial recognition, object detection, autonomous vehicles.

6. **Marketing:**

   - Customer segmentation, personalized advertising, churn prediction.

Popular Machine Learning Libraries and Frameworks

1. **Scikit-learn:**

   - A Python library for classical ML algorithms (e.g., regression, classification, clustering).

2. **TensorFlow and PyTorch:**

   - Frameworks for building and training deep learning models.

3. **Keras:**

   - A high-level API for building neural networks, often used with TensorFlow.

4. **Pandas and NumPy:**

   - Libraries for data manipulation and numerical computations.

5. **Matplotlib and Seaborn:**

   - Libraries for data visualization.

6. **XGBoost and LightGBM:**

   - Libraries for gradient boosting algorithms.

Challenges in Machine Learning

1. **Data Quality:**

   - Poor-quality data can lead to inaccurate models.

2. **Overfitting:**

   - When a model performs well on training data but poorly on unseen data.

3. **Scalability:**

   - Handling large datasets and complex models can be computationally expensive.

4. **Interpretability:**

   - Some models (e.g., deep learning) are difficult to interpret, making it hard to explain their decisions.

5. **Ethical Concerns:**

   - Bias in data and models can lead to unfair or discriminatory outcomes.

Future of Machine Learning

- **Automated Machine Learning (AutoML):** Tools that automate the process of model selection, hyperparameter tuning, and deployment.
- **Explainable AI (XAI):** Techniques to make ML models more transparent and interpretable.
- **Edge AI:** Deploying ML models on edge devices (e.g., smartphones, IoT devices) for real-time processing.
- **AI Ethics:** Developing frameworks to ensure fairness, accountability, and transparency in ML systems.

## CHAPTER TWO

Learning machine learning

Learning machine learning (ML) can seem daunting at first, but with a structured approach, you can build a strong foundation and gradually advance your skills. Here's a step-by-step guide to help you get started:

1. Understand the Basics

- **Prerequisites:**

  - **Mathematics**: Focus on linear algebra, calculus, probability, and statistics. These are essential for understanding ML algorithms.
  - **Programming**: Learn Python, the most widely used language in ML. Familiarize yourself with libraries like NumPy, pandas, and matplotlib.
  - **Data Handling**: Learn how to work with data (cleaning, preprocessing, and visualization).

- **Resources:**

  - Khan Academy (for math basics)
  - Python for Data Science Handbook by Jake VanderPlas
  - "Think Stats" by Allen B. Downey (for probability and statistics)

2. Learn the Fundamentals of Machine Learning

- **Key Concepts:**

  - Supervised learning (regression, classification)
  - Unsupervised learning (clustering, dimensionality reduction)
  - Model evaluation (accuracy, precision, recall, F1-score, etc.)

- ○ Overfitting and underfitting
- ○ Bias-variance tradeoff

- **Resources:**

  - ○ **Books:**

    - "Hands-On Machine Learning with Scikit-Learn, Keras, and TensorFlow" by Aurélien Géron
    - "Pattern Recognition and Machine Learning" by Christopher Bishop

  - ○ **Courses:**

    - Andrew Ng's Machine Learning course on Coursera (highly recommended for beginners)
    - Google's Machine Learning Crash Course

3. Practice with Real-World Data

- Work on datasets from platforms like:

  - ○ Kaggle (great for competitions and datasets)
  - ○ UCI Machine Learning Repository
  - ○ Google Dataset Search

- Start with simple projects like:

  - ○ Predicting house prices (regression)
  - ○ Classifying spam emails (classification)
  - ○ Clustering customer data (unsupervised learning)

4. Learn Advanced Topics

- **Deep Learning:** Study neural networks, convolutional neural networks (CNNs), recurrent neural networks (RNNs), and transformers.

- ◦ Resources: "Deep Learning" by Ian Goodfellow, Deep Learning Specialization by Andrew Ng on Coursera.

- **Natural Language Processing (NLP)**: Learn about text preprocessing, word embeddings, and language models.
- **Reinforcement Learning**: Explore Q-learning, policy gradients, and deep reinforcement learning.

5. Use ML Libraries and Frameworks

- **Scikit-learn**: For traditional ML algorithms.
- **TensorFlow** and **PyTorch**: For deep learning.
- **Keras**: High-level API for building neural networks.
- **XGBoost** and **LightGBM**: For gradient boosting.

6. Build Projects

- Apply your knowledge by building end-to-end projects. Examples:

  - ◦ Image classification using CNNs.
  - ◦ Sentiment analysis on social media data.
  - ◦ Recommendation systems for movies or products.

- Deploy your models using tools like Flask, FastAPI, or Streamlit.

7. Stay Updated and Engage with the Community

- Follow ML blogs, research papers, and conferences (e.g., NeurIPS, ICML).
- Join online communities like:

  - ◦ Kaggle forums
  - ◦ Reddit's r/MachineLearning
  - ◦ Stack Overflow

- Contribute to open-source ML projects on GitHub.

8. Specialize

- Once you have a solid foundation, choose a specialization:

  - Computer vision
  - NLP
  - Reinforcement learning
  - Generative AI (e.g., GANs, diffusion models)
  - Time series analysis

9. Practice, Practice, Practice

- Machine learning is a hands-on field. The more you practice, the better you'll get.
- Participate in Kaggle competitions to test your skills against others.

10. Learn from Mistakes

- Debugging and improving models is a key part of ML. Learn from errors and iterate.

Sample Learning Path:

1. **Month 1-2**: Learn Python, math basics, and data handling.
2. **Month 3-4**: Take Andrew Ng's ML course and work on small projects.
3. **Month 5-6**: Dive into deep learning and advanced topics.
4. **Month 7+**: Build and deploy projects, participate in competitions, and specialize.

WHY LINEAR ALGEBRA TO BE LEARNED FOR MACHINE LEARNING

Linear algebra is a fundamental mathematical tool in machine learning (ML) because it provides the language and framework for understanding and working with data, models, and algorithms. Here's why linear algebra is essential for ML and how it is used:

1. Data Representation

- **Vectors and Matrices**: Data in ML is often represented as vectors (for single data points) or matrices (for datasets). For example:

- A single image can be represented as a vector of pixel values.
- A dataset of images can be represented as a matrix, where each row corresponds to an image.

- Linear algebra provides the tools to manipulate and analyze these data structures efficiently.

2. Model Inputs and Outputs

- Many ML models, such as linear regression, neural networks, and support vector machines, rely on linear algebra to compute inputs and outputs.
- For example:

  - In linear regression, the model's predictions are computed as a weighted sum of input features (a dot product between vectors).
  - In neural networks, each layer's output is computed using matrix multiplications and activation functions.

3. Optimization

- ML involves optimizing objective functions (e.g., minimizing loss functions). Linear algebra is used to compute gradients, which are essential for optimization algorithms like gradient descent.
- For example:

  - The gradient of a loss function with respect to model parameters is often computed using matrix calculus.

4. Dimensionality Reduction

- Techniques like Principal Component Analysis (PCA) and Singular Value Decomposition (SVD) rely heavily on linear algebra to reduce the dimensionality of data while preserving its structure.
- These methods are used to simplify datasets, remove noise, and improve model performance.

5. Eigenvalues and Eigenvectors

- Eigenvalues and eigenvectors are used in many ML algorithms, such as PCA, to identify the most important directions (components) in the data.
- They are also used in spectral clustering and other advanced techniques.

6. Neural Networks

- Neural networks are built on linear algebra operations:

  - Forward propagation involves matrix multiplications and additions.
  - Backpropagation (used to train the network) relies on matrix derivatives and chain rule computations.

- Convolutional Neural Networks (CNNs) use convolution operations, which are also based on linear algebra.

7. Kernel Methods

- Algorithms like Support Vector Machines (SVMs) use kernel functions to transform data into higher-dimensional spaces. These transformations are based on linear algebra concepts like inner products and dot products.

8. Efficient Computations

- Linear algebra enables efficient computation of large-scale ML problems. Libraries like NumPy, TensorFlow, and PyTorch are optimized to perform linear algebra operations quickly, even on GPUs.

Key Linear Algebra Concepts for ML:

- **Vectors and Matrices:** Representing data and transformations.
- **Dot Products and Matrix Multiplication:** Used in model predictions and transformations.
- **Eigenvalues and Eigenvectors:** For dimensionality reduction and understanding data structure.
- **Singular Value Decomposition (SVD):** For matrix factorization and dimensionality reduction.

- **Matrix Inversion and Determinants**: Used in solving systems of equations and understanding transformations.
- **Gradients and Derivatives**: For optimization and training models.

Example Applications in ML:

1. **Linear Regression:**

   - The model is represented as $y=X\beta$, where X is the input matrix, β is the parameter vector, and y is the output.
   - Solving for β involves matrix operations like inversion and multiplication.

2. **Neural Networks:**

   - Each layer's output is computed as $z=Wx+b$, where W is a weight matrix, x is the input vector, and b is a bias vector.

3. **PCA:**

   - PCA involves computing eigenvectors of the covariance matrix to identify the principal components of the data.

WHY CALCULUS TO BE LEARNED FOR MACHINE LEARNING

Calculus is a critical mathematical foundation for machine learning (ML) because it provides the tools to understand and optimize the behavior of models. Many ML algorithms rely on calculus to make predictions, learn from data, and improve performance. Here's why calculus is essential for ML and how it is used:

1. Optimization

- **Core of ML:** Machine learning is all about optimizing models to minimize errors (loss functions) or maximize performance metrics.
- **Gradient Descent:** The most common optimization algorithm in ML, gradient descent, uses calculus to find the minimum of a loss function. It involves computing the gradient (derivative) of the loss function with respect to the model parameters and updating the parameters iteratively.

- Example: In linear regression, the goal is to minimize the mean squared error (MSE) by adjusting the model's weights. Calculus helps compute the derivatives of the MSE with respect to the weights.

2. Understanding Model Behavior

- **Derivatives**: Derivatives describe how a function changes as its inputs change. In ML, derivatives help us understand how small changes in model parameters (e.g., weights in a neural network) affect the output.
- **Partial Derivatives**: Many ML models have multiple parameters, so partial derivatives are used to compute the gradient with respect to each parameter.

3. Backpropagation in Neural Networks

- **Training Neural Networks**: Backpropagation, the algorithm used to train neural networks, relies heavily on calculus. It involves:

  1. Computing the error at the output layer.
  2. Propagating the error backward through the network using the chain rule of calculus.
  3. Updating the weights using gradients.

- Without calculus, it would be impossible to efficiently train deep learning models.

4. Loss Functions

- **Designing Loss Functions**: Calculus helps in designing and analyzing loss functions, which measure how well a model is performing.
- Example: In classification tasks, the cross-entropy loss function is used. Calculus helps compute its gradient, which is necessary for optimization.

5. Regularization

- **Preventing Overfitting**: Techniques like L1 and L2 regularization add penalty terms to the loss function to prevent overfitting. Calculus is used to compute the gradients of these penalty terms during optimization.

6. Probability and Statistics

- **Probabilistic Models**: Many ML models, such as Gaussian Mixture Models (GMMs) and Bayesian networks, are based on probability distributions. Calculus is used to compute integrals and derivatives for these distributions.
- Example: In maximum likelihood estimation (MLE), calculus is used to find the parameters that maximize the likelihood function.

7. Support Vector Machines (SVMs)

- **Optimization in SVMs**: SVMs involve solving a constrained optimization problem to find the optimal hyperplane. Calculus is used to derive the solution using Lagrange multipliers.

8. Gradient-Based Algorithms

- Many advanced optimization algorithms, such as Adam, RMSprop, and Adagrad, are based on gradients (computed using calculus). These algorithms are used to train deep learning models efficiently.

Key Calculus Concepts for ML:

- **Derivatives**: To understand how functions change and to compute gradients.
- **Partial Derivatives**: For functions with multiple variables (e.g., loss functions with multiple parameters).
- **Chain Rule**: For computing derivatives of composite functions (e.g., in backpropagation).
- **Gradients**: A vector of partial derivatives, used in optimization.
- **Integrals**: For computing expectations and probabilities in probabilistic models.
- **Convexity**: To analyze optimization problems and ensure they have a unique solution.

Example Applications in ML:

1. **Linear Regression:**

- ○ The loss function (e.g., mean squared error) is minimized using gradient descent, which requires computing derivatives.

2. **Neural Networks:**

   - ○ Backpropagation uses the chain rule to compute gradients for each layer.

3. **Logistic Regression:**

   - ○ The gradient of the log-loss function is computed to update the model parameters.

4. **Reinforcement Learning:**

   - ○ Policy gradient methods use calculus to optimize policies by computing gradients of expected rewards.

Resources to Learn Calculus for ML:

- **Books:**

  - ○ "Calculus" by James Stewart
  - ○ "Mathematics for Machine Learning" by Marc Peter Deisenroth, A. Aldo Faisal, and Cheng Soon Ong

- **Courses:**

  - ○ Khan Academy's Calculus course
  - ○ MIT OpenCourseWare's Single and Multivariable Calculus courses

- **Interactive Tools:**

  - ○ 3Blue1Brown's "Essence of Calculus" YouTube series (visual and intuitive explanations).

Why Calculus Matters:

- **Foundation for Optimization**: Calculus is the backbone of optimization, which is at the heart of ML.
- **Understanding Algorithms**: Without calculus, it's difficult to understand how algorithms like gradient descent, backpropagation, and SVMs work.
- **Building Intuition**: Calculus helps you develop intuition about how small changes in inputs or parameters affect outputs, which is crucial for debugging and improving models.

In summary, calculus is essential for machine learning because it enables optimization, helps in understanding and training models, and provides the mathematical tools to analyze and improve algorithms. If you want to dive deep into ML, a solid understanding of calculus is non-negotiable.

PROBABILITY AND STATISTICS

Probability and statistics are foundational to machine learning (ML) because they provide the tools to understand data, model uncertainty, and make informed decisions. ML algorithms are often built on probabilistic frameworks, and statistical methods are used to analyze data, evaluate models, and draw meaningful conclusions. Here's why probability and statistics are essential for ML and how they are applied:

1. Understanding Data

- **Data Distribution**: Probability helps describe the distribution of data, which is crucial for understanding patterns and making predictions.

  - Example: Knowing whether data follows a normal distribution, binomial distribution, or another distribution can guide the choice of ML models.

- **Descriptive Statistics**: Statistics provides tools like mean, median, variance, and standard deviation to summarize and analyze data.

2. Modeling Uncertainty

- **Probabilistic Models**: Many ML models, such as Bayesian networks, Gaussian Mixture Models (GMMs), and Hidden Markov Models (HMMs), are based on probability theory.

- **Uncertainty Quantification**: Probability allows ML models to express uncertainty in predictions (e.g., confidence intervals or posterior probabilities).

3. Inference and Prediction

- **Bayesian Inference**: Bayesian methods use probability to update beliefs (model parameters) based on observed data.

  - Example: In spam detection, Bayesian classifiers compute the probability that an email is spam given its features.

- **Maximum Likelihood Estimation (MLE)**: A statistical method used to estimate model parameters by maximizing the likelihood of the observed data.

4. Evaluating Models

- **Hypothesis Testing**: Statistics provides tools to test hypotheses about data or model performance.

  - Example: Testing whether a new model performs significantly better than an existing one.

- **Confidence Intervals**: Used to quantify the uncertainty in model predictions or parameter estimates.
- **P-values**: Help determine the significance of results.

5. Handling Noise and Variability

- **Noise in Data**: Real-world data is often noisy and incomplete. Probability and statistics help model and account for this noise.
- **Overfitting and Underfitting**: Statistical methods like cross-validation and regularization help prevent overfitting (modeling noise) and underfitting (oversimplifying the model).

6. Feature Engineering

- **Correlation and Dependence**: Statistics helps identify relationships between features (e.g., correlation coefficients) and remove redundant or irrelevant features.
- **Dimensionality Reduction**: Techniques like Principal Component Analysis (PCA) rely on statistical properties of data to reduce dimensionality.

7. Decision Making

- **Expected Value**: Probability helps compute the expected value of outcomes, which is useful in decision-making tasks (e.g., reinforcement learning).
- **Risk Assessment**: Statistics helps quantify risks and uncertainties in predictions.

8. Probabilistic ML Algorithms

- Many ML algorithms are inherently probabilistic:

  - **Naive Bayes**: A probabilistic classifier based on Bayes' theorem.
  - **Gaussian Processes**: Used for regression and classification, modeling data as a distribution over functions.
  - **Markov Chains and HMMs**: Used in sequence modeling (e.g., speech recognition, bioinformatics).

9. A/B Testing and Experimentation

- **A/B Testing**: Statistics is used to compare the performance of different models or strategies in real-world experiments.
- **Statistical Significance**: Ensures that observed differences are not due to random chance.

Key Probability and Statistics Concepts for ML:

- **Probability Basics:**

  - Probability rules, conditional probability, Bayes' theorem.

- **Distributions:**

  - Normal, binomial, Poisson, exponential, and other common distributions.

- **Expectation and Variance:**

  - Measures of central tendency and spread.

- **Statistical Inference:**

  - Hypothesis testing, confidence intervals, p-values.

- **Regression Analysis:**

  - Linear regression, logistic regression, and their assumptions.

- **Sampling and Estimation:**

  - Sampling methods, maximum likelihood estimation (MLE), Bayesian estimation.

- **Correlation and Causation:**

  - Understanding relationships between variables.

Example Applications in ML:

1. **Classification:**

   - Naive Bayes classifiers use probability to predict class labels.
   - Logistic regression models the probability of belonging to a class.

2. **Clustering:**

   - Gaussian Mixture Models (GMMs) use probability distributions to model clusters.

3. **Reinforcement Learning**:

   - Policies are often probabilistic, and decisions are based on expected rewards.

4. **Natural Language Processing (NLP)**:

   - Language models (e.g., n-grams, transformers) use probability to predict the next word in a sequence.

5. **Anomaly Detection**:

   - Statistical methods are used to identify outliers or unusual patterns in data.

Resources to Learn Probability and Statistics for ML:

- **Books:**

  - "Probability and Statistics" by Morris H. DeGroot and Mark J. Schervish.
  - "Think Stats" by Allen B. Downey (free online).
  - "Elements of Statistical Learning" by Trevor Hastie, Robert Tibshirani, and Jerome Friedman.

- **Courses:**

  - Khan Academy's Probability and Statistics courses.
  - "Statistical Thinking for Data Science and Analytics" by edX.

- **Interactive Tools:**

  - 3Blue1Brown's "Probability" YouTube series (visual explanations).

Why Probability and Statistics Matter:

- **Data-Driven Decisions:** ML is about making decisions based on data, and probability/statistics provide the framework for doing so.

- **Uncertainty Handling**: Real-world data is noisy and uncertain; probability helps model and manage this uncertainty.
- **Model Evaluation**: Statistics provides tools to evaluate and compare models rigorously.
- **Foundational Understanding**: Many ML algorithms (e.g., Bayesian methods, probabilistic graphical models) are built on probability and statistics.

In summary, probability and statistics are essential for machine learning because they enable data analysis, uncertainty modeling, and informed decision-making. Without a solid understanding of these concepts, it would be difficult to build, evaluate, and interpret ML models effectively.

WHY PYTHON TO BE LEARNED FOR MACHINE LEARNING

Python is the most popular programming language for machine learning (ML) and data science, and for good reason. Its simplicity, versatility, and extensive ecosystem of libraries and tools make it the go-to choice for both beginners and experts in the field. Here's why Python is essential for machine learning and how it is used:

1. Ease of Learning and Use

- **Beginner-Friendly**: Python has a simple and readable syntax, making it easy to learn for beginners.
- **Rapid Prototyping**: Python allows you to quickly implement and test ML ideas without getting bogged down by complex syntax or boilerplate code.

2. Extensive Libraries and Frameworks

Python has a rich ecosystem of libraries and frameworks specifically designed for machine learning and data science. Some of the most popular ones include:

- **NumPy**: For numerical computations and working with arrays.
- **pandas**: For data manipulation and analysis.
- **Matplotlib** and **Seaborn**: For data visualization.
- **Scikit-learn**: For traditional ML algorithms (e.g., regression, classification, clustering).
- **TensorFlow** and **PyTorch**: For deep learning.
- **Keras**: A high-level API for building neural networks.

- **XGBoost** and **LightGBM**: For gradient boosting algorithms.
- **NLTK** and **spaCy**: For natural language processing (NLP).
- **OpenCV**: For computer vision tasks.

3. Community Support

- **Large Community**: Python has one of the largest and most active communities in the world. This means you can easily find tutorials, documentation, and help online.
- **Open Source**: Most Python libraries are open source, meaning they are free to use and continuously improved by the community.

4. Integration with Other Tools

- **Data Handling**: Python integrates seamlessly with databases, big data tools (e.g., Apache Spark), and cloud platforms (e.g., AWS, Google Cloud, Azure).
- **Web Frameworks**: Python can be used with web frameworks like Flask and Django to deploy ML models as web services.
- **Jupyter Notebooks**: An interactive environment for writing and sharing code, visualizations, and explanations. It's widely used in data science and ML.

5. Versatility

- Python is a general-purpose language, meaning it can be used for a wide range of tasks beyond ML, such as web development, automation, and scripting.
- This versatility makes it a one-stop solution for end-to-end ML projects, from data collection and preprocessing to model deployment.

6. Cross-Platform Compatibility

- Python runs on all major operating systems (Windows, macOS, Linux), making it easy to share and collaborate on projects across different platforms.

7. Support for Research and Production

- **Research**: Python is widely used in academia and research due to its simplicity and the availability of libraries like SciPy and SymPy.
- **Production**: Python is also used in industry for building scalable ML systems. Tools like TensorFlow Serving and FastAPI make it easy to deploy ML models in production.

8. Machine Learning Workflow

Python supports every step of the ML workflow:

1. **Data Collection**: Libraries like requests and BeautifulSoup for web scraping, or pandas for reading data from files.
2. **Data Cleaning and Preprocessing**: pandas and NumPy for handling missing data, scaling, and encoding.
3. **Exploratory Data Analysis (EDA)**: Matplotlib, Seaborn, and pandas for visualizing and understanding data.
4. **Model Building**: Scikit-learn, TensorFlow, and PyTorch for training ML models.
5. **Model Evaluation**: Scikit-learn for metrics like accuracy, precision, recall, and F1-score.
6. **Model Deployment**: Flask, FastAPI, or Django for deploying models as APIs.

9. Industry Adoption

- Python is the language of choice for many tech giants and startups in the ML space, including Google, Facebook, Amazon, and Netflix.
- This widespread adoption means that learning Python opens up numerous career opportunities in data science and ML.

10. Learning Resources

- Python has an abundance of free and paid resources for learning ML, including:

    - Online courses (e.g., Coursera, edX, Udemy).
    - Books (e.g., "Python Machine Learning" by Sebastian Raschka).
    - Tutorials and documentation (e.g., official Python docs, Kaggle tutorials).

◦ Community forums (e.g., Stack Overflow, Reddit).

Example Use Cases of Python in ML:

1. **Image Classification:**

   ◦ Using TensorFlow or PyTorch to build convolutional neural networks (CNNs) for tasks like identifying objects in images.

2. **Natural Language Processing (NLP):**

   ◦ Using libraries like NLTK, spaCy, or Hugging Face Transformers for tasks like sentiment analysis or text generation.

3. **Recommendation Systems:**

   ◦ Using Scikit-learn or TensorFlow to build collaborative filtering or content-based recommendation systems.

4. **Time Series Forecasting:**

   ◦ Using libraries like statsmodels or Prophet to predict future trends based on historical data.

5. **Anomaly Detection:**

   ◦ Using Scikit-learn or PyOD to identify unusual patterns in data.

Why Python is the Best Choice for ML:

- **Accessibility:** Easy to learn and use, even for non-programmers.
- **Ecosystem:** A vast collection of libraries and tools for every stage of the ML pipeline.
- **Community:** Strong support from a large and active community.
- **Flexibility:** Suitable for both research and production environments.
- **Industry Standard:** Widely adopted in academia and industry.

Getting Started with Python for ML:

1. **Learn Python Basics:**

   ◦ Variables, loops, functions, and data structures (lists, dictionaries, etc.).

2. **Explore Data Science Libraries:**

   ◦ Start with NumPy, pandas, and Matplotlib.

3. **Learn ML Libraries:**

   ◦ Begin with Scikit-learn for traditional ML, then move to TensorFlow or PyTorch for deep learning.

4. **Work on Projects:**

   ◦ Apply your skills to real-world datasets and problems (e.g., Kaggle competitions).

5. **Deploy Models:**

   ◦ Learn how to deploy ML models using Flask, FastAPI, or cloud platforms.

In summary, Python is the most widely used language for machine learning because of its simplicity, versatility, and powerful ecosystem of libraries and tools. Whether you're a beginner or an expert, Python provides everything you need to build, evaluate, and deploy ML models effectively.

## CHAPTER THREE

Different types of AI

1. Types of AI Based on Capabilities

AI systems can be classified based on their ability to mimic human intelligence and perform tasks.

a) Narrow AI (Weak AI)

- Definition: AI designed to perform a specific task or a narrow range of tasks.
- Characteristics:

  - Excels at one task but cannot generalize to other tasks.
  - Does not possess consciousness or self-awareness.

- Examples:

  - Voice assistants (e.g., Siri, Alexa).
  - Image recognition systems.
  - Recommendation systems (e.g., Netflix, Amazon).

b) General AI (Strong AI)

- Definition: AI that can perform any intellectual task that a human can do.
- Characteristics:

  - Possesses human-like reasoning, problem-solving, and learning abilities.
  - Can generalize knowledge across domains.
  - Still theoretical and does not exist yet.

- Examples:

  - Hypothetical systems that can think and reason like humans.

c) Superintelligent AI

- Definition: AI that surpasses human intelligence in all aspects.
- Characteristics:

  - Capable of outperforming humans in creativity, problem-solving, and decision-making.
  - Exists only in science fiction and theoretical discussions.

- Examples:

  - Hypothetical systems like Skynet (from *Terminator*) or HAL 9000 (from *2001: A Space Odyssey*).

2. Types of AI Based on Functionality

AI systems can also be classified based on their functionality and how they mimic human behavior.

a) Reactive Machines

- Definition: AI systems that react to specific inputs without memory or past experiences.
- Characteristics:

  - Cannot learn from past data or experiences.
  - Operates based on predefined rules.

- Examples:

  - IBM's Deep Blue (chess-playing AI).
  - Spam filters.

b) Limited Memory AI

- Definition: AI systems that use past experiences (data) to make decisions.
- Characteristics:

  - Can learn from historical data to improve performance.
  - Most current AI systems fall into this category.

- Examples:

  - Self-driving cars (use past data to navigate).
  - Chatbots (learn from past conversations).

c) Theory of Mind AI

- Definition: AI systems that can understand emotions, beliefs, and intentions of others.
- Characteristics:

  - Can interact socially and emotionally with humans.
  - Still in the research phase.

- Examples:

  - Hypothetical AI systems that can understand human emotions and respond appropriately.

d) Self-Aware AI

- Definition: AI systems that possess self-awareness and consciousness.
- Characteristics:

  - Can understand its own existence and emotions.
  - Purely theoretical and not yet achieved.

- Examples:

  - Hypothetical systems like robots with human-like consciousness.

3. Types of AI Based on Techniques

AI can also be categorized based on the techniques and methodologies used to build intelligent systems.

a) Rule-Based AI (Symbolic AI)

- Definition: AI systems that use predefined rules and logic to make decisions.
- Characteristics:

  - Relies on human expertise to create rules.
  - Limited ability to handle uncertainty or learn from data.

- Examples:

  - Expert systems (e.g., medical diagnosis systems).
  - Business rule engines.

b) Machine Learning (ML)

- Definition: AI systems that learn patterns from data without being explicitly programmed.
- Characteristics:

  - Uses algorithms to identify patterns and make predictions.
  - Can improve performance with more data.

- Examples:

  - Supervised learning (e.g., classification, regression).
  - Unsupervised learning (e.g., clustering, dimensionality reduction).
  - Reinforcement learning (e.g., game-playing AI).

c) Deep Learning (DL)

- Definition: A subset of machine learning that uses neural networks with many layers.
- Characteristics:

- Excels at processing unstructured data (e.g., images, text, audio).
- Requires large amounts of data and computational power.

- Examples:

  - Convolutional Neural Networks (CNNs) for image recognition.
  - Recurrent Neural Networks (RNNs) for natural language processing.

d) Natural Language Processing (NLP)

- Definition: AI systems that enable machines to understand, interpret, and generate human language.
- Characteristics:

  - Combines linguistics, computer science, and machine learning.
  - Used for text and speech-based applications.

- Examples:

  - Chatbots (e.g., ChatGPT).
  - Language translation (e.g., Google Translate).
  - Sentiment analysis.

e) Computer Vision

- Definition: AI systems that enable machines to interpret and understand visual data.
- Characteristics:

  - Uses techniques like image processing and deep learning.
  - Can recognize objects, faces, and scenes.

- Examples:

  - Facial recognition systems.
  - Autonomous vehicles (e.g., Tesla's Autopilot).

f) Robotics

- Definition: AI systems integrated into physical machines (robots) to perform tasks.
- Characteristics:

  - Combines AI with mechanical engineering.
  - Used for automation and physical interaction.

- Examples:

  - Industrial robots (e.g., assembly line robots).
  - Service robots (e.g., Roomba vacuum cleaners).

4. Types of AI Based on Learning Methods
AI systems can also be classified based on how they learn from data.
a) Supervised Learning

- Definition: AI systems trained on labeled data (input-output pairs).
- Characteristics:

  - Learns to map inputs to outputs.
  - Used for tasks like classification and regression.

- Examples:

  - Predicting house prices (regression).
  - Classifying emails as spam or not spam (classification).

b) Unsupervised Learning

- Definition: AI systems trained on unlabeled data to find patterns.
- Characteristics:

  - Used for tasks like clustering and dimensionality reduction.

- Examples:

  - Grouping customers based on purchasing behavior (clustering).

- ○ Reducing the number of features in a dataset (dimensionality reduction).

c) Reinforcement Learning

- Definition: AI systems that learn by interacting with an environment and receiving rewards or penalties.
- Characteristics:

  - ○ Used for decision-making tasks.
  - ○ Learns through trial and error.

- Examples:

  - ○ Game-playing AI (e.g., AlphaGo).
  - ○ Robotics (e.g., training robots to walk).

5. Types of AI Based on Applications
AI can also be categorized based on its real-world applications.
a) Healthcare AI

- Examples:

  - ○ Disease diagnosis (e.g., cancer detection).
  - ○ Drug discovery.
  - ○ Personalized medicine.

b) Financial AI

- Examples:

  - ○ Fraud detection.
  - ○ Algorithmic trading.
  - ○ Credit scoring.

c) Retail AI

- Examples:

- ○ Recommendation systems (e.g., Amazon, Netflix).
- ○ Inventory management.
- ○ Customer service chatbots.

d) Autonomous Systems

- Examples:

  - ○ Self-driving cars (e.g., Tesla, Waymo).
  - ○ Drones.
  - ○ Industrial automation.

e) Entertainment AI

- Examples:

  - ○ Video game AI.
  - ○ Content recommendation (e.g., YouTube, Spotify).
  - ○ Deepfake technology.

## CHAPTER FOUR

Commonly used Python Libraries in Machine Learning

Python has a rich ecosystem of libraries that are widely used in machine learning (ML) and data science. Below is a list of **commonly used Python libraries** in ML, along with examples of how they are used:

1. NumPy

- **Purpose**: Numerical computing and working with arrays.
- **Use Case**: Efficiently handle large datasets and perform mathematical operations.
- **Example**:

```python
Copy
import numpy as np
# Create a numpy array
data = np.array([[1, 2], [3, 4]])
# Perform matrix multiplication
result = np.dot(data, data.T)
print(result)
```

2. pandas

- **Purpose**: Data manipulation and analysis.
- **Use Case**: Clean, preprocess, and analyze structured data (e.g., CSV files, Excel sheets).
- **Example**:

```python
```

```
Copy
import pandas as pd
# Load a dataset
data = pd.read_csv('data.csv')
# Display the first 5 rows
print(data.head())
# Calculate the mean of a column
print(data['column_name'].mean())
```

3. Matplotlib

- **Purpose**: Data visualization.
- **Use Case**: Create plots and charts to explore and present data.
- **Example**:

```python
Copy
import matplotlib.pyplot as plt
# Create a simple line plot
x = [1, 2, 3, 4]
y = [10, 20, 25, 30]
plt.plot(x, y)
plt.xlabel('X-axis')
plt.ylabel('Y-axis')
plt.title('Simple Line Plot')
plt.show()
```

4. Scikit-learn

- **Purpose**: Traditional machine learning algorithms.
- **Use Case**: Implement regression, classification, clustering, and more.
- **Example**:

```python
Copy
from sklearn.datasets import load_iris
from sklearn.model_selection import train_test_split
from sklearn.ensemble import RandomForestClassifier
from sklearn.metrics import accuracy_score
# Load dataset
```

```python
data = load_iris()
X_train, X_test, y_train, y_test = train_test_split(data.data, data.target,
test_size=0.2)
# Train a Random Forest model
model = RandomForestClassifier()
model.fit(X_train, y_train)
# Make predictions
predictions = model.predict(X_test)
print("Accuracy:", accuracy_score(y_test, predictions))
```

5. TensorFlow

- **Purpose**: Deep learning and neural networks.
- **Use Case**: Build and train complex models like CNNs, RNNs, and transformers.
- **Example**:

```python
python
Copy
import tensorflow as tf
from tensorflow.keras import layers
# Build a simple neural network
model = tf.keras.Sequential([
layers.Dense(64, activation='relu', input_shape=(10,)),
layers.Dense(1)
])
# Compile the model
model.compile(optimizer='adam', loss='mse')
# Train the model
model.fit(X_train, y_train, epochs=10)
```

6. PyTorch

- **Purpose**: Deep learning and research.
- **Use Case**: Build and train custom neural networks with flexibility.
- **Example**:

```python
python
Copy
import torch
```

```python
import torch.nn as nn
import torch.optim as optim
# Define a simple neural network
class Net(nn.Module):
def __init__(self):
super(Net, self).__init__()
self.fc1 = nn.Linear(10, 64)
self.fc2 = nn.Linear(64, 1)
def forward(self, x):
x = torch.relu(self.fc1(x))
return self.fc2(x)
# Initialize the model, loss function, and optimizer
model = Net()
criterion = nn.MSELoss()
optimizer = optim.Adam(model.parameters(), lr=0.001)
# Training loop
for epoch in range(10):
outputs = model(X_train)
loss = criterion(outputs, y_train)
optimizer.zero_grad()
loss.backward()
optimizer.step()
```

7. Keras

- **Purpose**: High-level deep learning API.
- **Use Case**: Quickly build and train neural networks.
- **Example**:

```python
python
Copy
from tensorflow.keras.models import Sequential
from tensorflow.keras.layers import Dense
# Build a simple model
model = Sequential([
Dense(64, activation='relu', input_shape=(10,)),
Dense(1)
])
# Compile and train
```

```
model.compile(optimizer='adam', loss='mse')
model.fit(X_train, y_train, epochs=10)
```

8. XGBoost

- **Purpose:** Gradient boosting for structured/tabular data.
- **Use Case:** Win Kaggle competitions and solve classification/regression problems.
- **Example:**

```python
Copy
import xgboost as xgb
from sklearn.datasets import load_boston
from sklearn.model_selection import train_test_split
# Load dataset
data = load_boston()
X_train, X_test, y_train, y_test = train_test_split(data.data, data.target, test_size=0.2)
# Train an XGBoost model
model = xgb.XGBRegressor()
model.fit(X_train, y_train)
# Make predictions
predictions = model.predict(X_test)
```

9. LightGBM

- **Purpose:** Gradient boosting with faster training and lower memory usage.
- **Use Case:** Handle large datasets efficiently.
- **Example:**

```python
Copy
import lightgbm as lgb
from sklearn.datasets import load_iris
from sklearn.model_selection import train_test_split
# Load dataset
data = load_iris()
```

```
X_train, X_test, y_train, y_test = train_test_split(data.data, data.target,
test_size=0.2)
# Train a LightGBM model
model = lgb.LGBMClassifier()
model.fit(X_train, y_train)
# Make predictions
predictions = model.predict(X_test)
```

10. NLTK and spaCy

- **Purpose**: Natural Language Processing (NLP).
- **Use Case**: Text preprocessing, tokenization, and sentiment analysis.
- **Example**:

```
python
Copy
import nltk
from nltk.tokenize import word_tokenize
# Tokenize text
text = "Hello, how are you?"
tokens = word_tokenize(text)
print(tokens)
```

11. OpenCV

- **Purpose**: Computer vision.
- **Use Case**: Image processing, object detection, and video analysis.
- **Example**:

```
python
Copy
import cv2
# Load an image
image = cv2.imread('image.jpg')
# Convert to grayscale
gray = cv2.cvtColor(image, cv2.COLOR_BGR2GRAY)
cv2.imshow('Grayscale Image', gray)
cv2.waitKey(0)
```

12. Seaborn

- **Purpose**: Statistical data visualization.
- **Use Case**: Create attractive and informative statistical plots.
- **Example**:

```python
python
Copy
import seaborn as sns
import matplotlib.pyplot as plt
# Load a dataset
tips = sns.load_dataset('tips')
# Create a boxplot
sns.boxplot(x='day', y='total_bill', data=tips)
plt.show()
```

13. Statsmodels

- **Purpose**: Statistical modeling and hypothesis testing.
- **Use Case**: Perform regression analysis and statistical tests.
- **Example**:

```python
python
Copy
import statsmodels.api as sm
import numpy as np
# Generate some data
X = np.random.rand(100, 2)
y = X[:, 0] + 2 * X[:, 1] + np.random.randn(100)
# Fit a linear regression model
model = sm.OLS(y, sm.add_constant(X))
results = model.fit()
print(results.summary())
```

14. Jupyter Notebooks

- **Purpose**: Interactive coding and data exploration.
- **Use Case**: Combine code, visualizations, and explanations in a single document.
- **Example**:

  - Install Jupyter: pip install jupyterlab

◦ Run: jupyter lab or jupyter notebook
◦ Write and execute Python code interactively.

Summary

These libraries form the backbone of machine learning in Python. By mastering them, you can handle every stage of the ML pipeline, from data preprocessing and visualization to model building, evaluation, and deployment.

Learn how to work with data (cleaning, preprocessing, and visualization in machine learning

Working with data is a fundamental part of machine learning (ML). It involves several steps, including cleaning, preprocessing, and visualization. Below is a guide to help you understand and implement these steps effectively:

1. Data Cleaning

Data cleaning involves handling missing, inconsistent, or incorrect data to ensure the dataset is ready for analysis and modeling.

Key Steps:

- **Handle Missing Values:**

  ◦ Remove rows or columns with too many missing values.
  ◦ Impute missing values using techniques like mean, median, mode, or advanced methods like KNN imputation.

```python
python
Copy
import pandas as pd
from sklearn.impute import SimpleImputer
# Example: Impute missing values with the mean
imputer = SimpleImputer(strategy='mean')
df['column_name'] = imputer.fit_transform(df[['column_name']])
```

- **Remove Duplicates:**

  ◦ Identify and drop duplicate rows.

```python
python
```

Copy
df.drop_duplicates(inplace=True)

- **Handle Outliers:**

    ◦ Detect outliers using statistical methods (e.g., Z-score, IQR).
    ◦ Remove or transform outliers based on the context.

python
Copy
```python
from scipy.stats import zscore
# Example: Remove rows with Z-score > 3
df = df[(zscore(df['column_name']) < 3)]
```

- **Correct Inconsistent Data:**

    ◦ Standardize categorical values (e.g., "Male" vs. "M").
    ◦ Fix typos and formatting issues.

2. Data Preprocessing

Data preprocessing transforms raw data into a format suitable for machine learning models.

Key Steps:

- **Feature Scaling:**

    ◦ Normalize or standardize numerical features to bring them to a similar scale.

python
Copy
```python
from sklearn.preprocessing import StandardScaler, MinMaxScaler
# Standardization
scaler = StandardScaler()
df['column_name'] = scaler.fit_transform(df[['column_name']])
# Normalization
scaler = MinMaxScaler()
df['column_name'] = scaler.fit_transform(df[['column_name']])
```

- **Encode Categorical Variables:**

  - Convert categorical data into numerical format using one-hot encoding or label encoding.

```python
Copy
from sklearn.preprocessing import OneHotEncoder, LabelEncoder
# One-hot encoding
df = pd.get_dummies(df, columns=['categorical_column'])
# Label encoding
label_encoder = LabelEncoder()
df['categorical_column'] = label_encoder.fit_transform(df['categorical_column'])
```

- **Feature Engineering:**

  - Create new features from existing ones (e.g., extracting year from a date).
  - Combine or split features as needed.

```python
Copy
# Example: Extract year from a date column
df['year'] = pd.to_datetime(df['date_column']).dt.year
```

- **Split Data:**

  - Divide the dataset into training, validation, and test sets.

```python
Copy
from sklearn.model_selection import train_test_split
X_train, X_test, y_train, y_test = train_test_split(X, y, test_size=0.2, random_state=42)
```

3. Data Visualization

Data visualization helps you understand the data distribution, relationships, and patterns.

Key Techniques:

- **Univariate Analysis:**

  - Visualize the distribution of a single variable using histograms, box plots, or density plots.

```python
python
Copy
import seaborn as sns
import matplotlib.pyplot as plt
# Histogram
sns.histplot(df['column_name'], kde=True)
plt.show()
# Box plot
sns.boxplot(df['column_name'])
plt.show()
```

- **Bivariate Analysis:**

  - Explore relationships between two variables using scatter plots, pair plots, or correlation heatmaps.

```python
python
Copy
# Scatter plot
sns.scatterplot(x='column1', y='column2', data=df)
plt.show()
# Correlation heatmap
sns.heatmap(df.corr(), annot=True, cmap='coolwarm')
plt.show()
```

- **Multivariate Analysis:**

  - Use pair plots or 3D plots to analyze relationships between multiple variables.

```python
python
```

Copy
# Pair plot
sns.pairplot(df)
plt.show()

- **Time Series Visualization:**

  - Use line plots to visualize trends over time.

python
Copy
plt.plot(df['date_column'], df['value_column'])
plt.xlabel('Date')
plt.ylabel('Value')
plt.show()

4. Tools and Libraries

- **Pandas**: For data manipulation and cleaning.
- **NumPy**: For numerical operations.
- **Scikit-learn**: For preprocessing and splitting data.
- **Matplotlib and Seaborn**: For data visualization.
- **Plotly**: For interactive visualizations.

5. Best Practices

- Always explore the data before cleaning and preprocessing.
- Document every step of the data preparation process.
- Validate the cleaned and preprocessed data to ensure it's ready for modeling.
- Use visualization to communicate insights effectively.

## CHAPTER FIVE

Label Data and Un-labeled Data

1. Labeled Data

Labeled data refers to data that includes both input features and the corresponding output (target variable). The "label" is the correct answer or outcome that the model is expected to predict.

Characteristics:

- Each data point has an input (features) and an output (label).
- Used in **supervised learning**, where the model learns to map inputs to outputs.
- Requires human effort to annotate or label the data.

Examples:

1. **Spam Detection:**

    ◦ Input: Email text.
    ◦ Label: "Spam" or "Not Spam."
    ◦ The model learns to classify emails based on labeled examples.

2. **House Price Prediction:**

    ◦ Input: Features like square footage, number of bedrooms, location.
    ◦ Label: Price of the house.
    ◦ The model learns to predict house prices based on historical data.

3. **Image Classification:**

- ○ Input: Images of cats and dogs.
- ○ Label: "Cat" or "Dog."
- ○ The model learns to classify images based on labeled examples.

4. **Medical Diagnosis:**

- ○ Input: Patient data (e.g., age, blood pressure, symptoms).
- ○ Label: Diagnosis (e.g., "Healthy" or "Diseased").
- ○ The model learns to predict diagnoses based on labeled patient records.

Advantages:

- Enables supervised learning, which often achieves high accuracy.
- Provides clear feedback to the model during training.

Challenges:

- Requires significant effort and cost to label data.
- May introduce human bias during the labeling process.

2. Unlabeled Data

Unlabeled data refers to data that only contains input features without any corresponding output labels. The model must find patterns or structures in the data on its own.

Characteristics:

- Only input features are available; no target variable is provided.
- Used in **unsupervised learning**, where the model identifies hidden patterns or groupings.
- Often more abundant and easier to collect than labeled data.

Examples:

1. **Customer Segmentation:**

- ○ Input: Customer purchase history, demographics, and behavior.
- ○ Label: None.

- ◦ The model clusters customers into groups based on similarities.

2. **Anomaly Detection:**

   - ◦ Input: Network traffic data.
   - ◦ Label: None.
   - ◦ The model identifies unusual patterns that may indicate cyberattacks.

3. **Topic Modeling:**

   - ◦ Input: Collection of text documents.
   - ◦ Label: None.
   - ◦ The model identifies common topics or themes in the documents.

4. **Image Clustering:**

   - ◦ Input: Collection of unlabeled images.
   - ◦ Label: None.
   - ◦ The model groups similar images together (e.g., photos of landscapes, animals).

Advantages:

- Easier and cheaper to collect since no labeling is required.
- Useful for exploratory data analysis and discovering hidden patterns.

Challenges:

- Harder to evaluate model performance since there are no ground truth labels.
- Requires domain expertise to interpret the results.

Comparison: Labeled vs. Unlabeled Data

Aspect	Labeled Data	Unlabeled Data
Definition	Data with input features and labels.	Data with only input features.
Usage	Supervised learning.	Unsupervised learning.
Examples	Spam detection, house price prediction.	Customer segmentation, anomaly detection.
Cost	Expensive and time-consuming to label.	Cheaper and easier to collect.
Model Feedback	Clear feedback during training.	No explicit feedback; relies on patterns.
Applications	Classification, regression.	Clustering, dimensionality reduction.

Comparison: Labeled vs. Unlabeled Data

## CHAPTER SIX

Tools and libraries

In machine learning projects, a variety of tools and libraries are used to streamline the development process, from data preprocessing to model deployment. Here's a list of commonly used tools and libraries, categorized by their purpose:

1. Data Preprocessing and Manipulation

- **Pandas:**

  - For data manipulation and analysis (e.g., handling missing data, filtering, grouping).
  - Website: pandas.pydata.org

- **NumPy:**

  - For numerical computations and array operations.
  - Website: numpy.org

- **OpenPyXL:**

  - For working with Excel files.
  - Website: openpyxl.readthedocs.io

2. Data Visualization

- **Matplotlib:**

  - For creating static, interactive, and animated visualizations.
  - Website: matplotlib.org

- **Seaborn:**

  - For statistical data visualization (built on top of Matplotlib).
  - Website: seaborn.pydata.org

- **Plotly:**

  - For interactive and web-based visualizations.
  - Website: plotly.com

- **Tableau:**

  - For creating interactive and shareable dashboards.
  - Website: tableau.com

3. Machine Learning Frameworks

- **Scikit-learn:**

  - For traditional machine learning algorithms (e.g., regression, classification, clustering).
  - Website: scikit-learn.org

- **TensorFlow:**

  - For deep learning and neural networks.
  - Website: tensorflow.org

- **PyTorch:**

  - For deep learning, with a focus on flexibility and dynamic computation graphs.
  - Website: pytorch.org

- **Keras:**

  - High-level API for building and training deep learning models (runs on top of TensorFlow).

- ○ Website: keras.io

4. Model Evaluation and Optimization

- **Scikit-learn:**

  - ○ Provides tools for model evaluation (e.g., cross-validation, metrics).

- **Hyperopt:**

  - ○ For hyperparameter tuning using Bayesian optimization.
  - ○ Website: hyperopt.github.io

- **Optuna:**

  - ○ For automated hyperparameter optimization.
  - ○ Website: optuna.org

- **MLflow:**

  - ○ For tracking experiments, packaging code, and deploying models.
  - ○ Website: mlflow.org

5. Natural Language Processing (NLP)

- **NLTK:**

  - ○ For text processing and analysis.
  - ○ Website: nltk.org

- **spaCy:**

  - ○ For industrial-strength NLP tasks.
  - ○ Website: spacy.io

- **Transformers (Hugging Face):**

  - ○ For state-of-the-art NLP models (e.g., BERT, GPT).

- ◦ Website: huggingface.co

- **Gensim:**

  - ◦ For topic modeling and document similarity analysis.
  - ◦ Website: radimrehurek.com/gensim

6. Time-Series Analysis

- **Statsmodels:**

  - ◦ For statistical modeling and time-series analysis (e.g., ARIMA).
  - ◦ Website: statsmodels.org

- **Prophet:**

  - ◦ For forecasting time-series data developed by Facebook.
  - ◦ Website: facebook.github.io/prophet

- **PyCaret:**

  - ◦ For automating time-series forecasting workflows.
  - ◦ Website: pycaret.org

7. Big Data and Distributed Computing

- **Apache Spark:**

  - ◦ For distributed data processing and machine learning.
  - ◦ Website: spark.apache.org

- **Dask:**

  - ◦ For parallel computing and scaling Python workflows.
  - ◦ Website: dask.org

- **Hadoop:**

- For distributed storage and processing of large datasets.
- Website: hadoop.apache.org

8. Model Deployment

- **Flask:**

  - For building web APIs to deploy machine learning models.
  - Website: flask.palletsprojects.com

- **FastAPI:**

  - For building high-performance web APIs.
  - Website: fastapi.tiangolo.com

- **Docker:**

  - For containerizing applications and ensuring consistency across environments.
  - Website: docker.com

- **Kubernetes:**

  - For orchestrating containerized applications.
  - Website: kubernetes.io

- **Streamlit:**

  - For building interactive web apps for machine learning models.
  - Website: streamlit.io

9. Version Control and Collaboration

- **Git:**

  - For version control and collaboration.
  - Website: git-scm.com

- **GitHub/GitLab:**

  - For hosting and sharing code repositories.
  - Websites: github.com, gitlab.com

- **DVC (Data Version Control):**

  - For versioning datasets and machine learning models.
  - Website: dvc.org

10. Cloud Platforms

- **AWS (Amazon Web Services):**

  - For cloud computing, storage, and machine learning services (e.g., SageMaker).
  - Website: aws.amazon.com

- **Google Cloud Platform (GCP):**

  - For cloud-based machine learning and data processing (e.g., AI Platform).
  - Website: cloud.google.com

- **Microsoft Azure:**

  - For cloud-based machine learning and AI services (e.g., Azure ML).
  - Website: azure.microsoft.com

11. Integrated Development Environments (IDEs)

- **Jupyter Notebook:**

  - For interactive coding and data exploration.
  - Website: jupyter.org

- **VS Code:**

- ○ A lightweight and powerful code editor with extensions for machine learning.
- ○ Website: code.visualstudio.com

- **PyCharm:**

  - ○ A Python-specific IDE with advanced debugging and development tools.
  - ○ Website: jetbrains.com/pycharm

12. Specialized Libraries

- **XGBoost, LightGBM, CatBoost:**

  - ○ For gradient boosting algorithms.
  - ○ Websites: xgboost.ai, lightgbm.readthedocs.io, catboost.ai

- **SHAP (SHapley Additive exPlanations):**

  - ○ For model interpretability and feature importance.
  - ○ Website: shap.readthedocs.io

- **Yellowbrick:**

  - ○ For visual diagnostics of machine learning models.
  - ○ Website: www.scikit-yb.org

Summary

- **Data Preprocessing:** Pandas, NumPy, OpenPyXL.
- **Data Visualization:** Matplotlib, Seaborn, Plotly, Tableau.
- **Machine Learning:** Scikit-learn, TensorFlow, PyTorch, Keras.
- **Model Evaluation:** Scikit-learn, Hyperopt, Optuna, MLflow.
- **NLP:** NLTK, spaCy, Transformers, Gensim.
- **Time-Series:** Statsmodels, Prophet, PyCaret.
- **Big Data:** Apache Spark, Dask, Hadoop.
- **Model Deployment:** Flask, FastAPI, Docker, Kubernetes, Streamlit.
- **Version Control:** Git, GitHub/GitLab, DVC.

- **Cloud Platforms**: AWS, GCP, Azure.
- **IDEs**: Jupyter Notebook, VS Code, PyCharm.
- **Specialized Libraries**: XGBoost, LightGBM, CatBoost, SHAP, Yellowbrick.

• 58 •

By leveraging these tools and libraries, you can efficiently develop, evaluate, and deploy machine learning models

## CHAPTER SEVEN

Different Types of Machine Learning

Machine learning (ML) is a subset of artificial intelligence (AI) that focuses on building systems that can learn from data and improve their performance over time without being explicitly programmed. Based on the nature of the learning process and the type of supervision required, machine learning can be broadly categorized into **three main types:**

1. Supervised Learning

Supervised learning is the most common type of machine learning, where the model is trained on a labeled dataset. The dataset consists of input-output pairs, where the input is the feature set, and the output is the corresponding label or target. The goal is to learn a mapping function from the input to the output so that the model can make accurate predictions on unseen data.

Key Characteristics:

- Requires labeled data (input-output pairs).
- The model learns to predict the output based on the input features.
- Commonly used for tasks where the relationship between inputs and outputs is well-defined.

Examples of Supervised Learning Tasks:

- **Classification:** Predicting discrete labels (e.g., spam detection, image classification).

  - Algorithms: Logistic Regression, Support Vector Machines (SVM), Decision Trees, Random Forests, Neural Networks.

- **Regression**: Predicting continuous values (e.g., house price prediction, stock price forecasting).

  - Algorithms: Linear Regression, Ridge Regression, Lasso Regression, Neural Networks.

Example:

- Predicting whether an email is spam (classification) or predicting the price of a house based on its features (regression).

2. Unsupervised Learning

Unsupervised learning involves training models on unlabeled data, where the goal is to discover hidden patterns, structures, or relationships within the data. Unlike supervised learning, there are no predefined labels or outputs.

Key Characteristics:

- Works with unlabeled data.
- Focuses on finding intrinsic structures or groupings in the data.
- Commonly used for exploratory data analysis and feature extraction.

Examples of Unsupervised Learning Tasks:

- **Clustering**: Grouping similar data points together (e.g., customer segmentation, document clustering).

  - Algorithms: K-Means, Hierarchical Clustering, DBSCAN, Gaussian Mixture Models (GMM).

- **Dimensionality Reduction**: Reducing the number of features while preserving important information (e.g., visualization, noise reduction).

  - Algorithms: Principal Component Analysis (PCA), t-SNE, UMAP.

- **Anomaly Detection**: Identifying rare or unusual data points (e.g., fraud detection, network intrusion detection).

- ◦ Algorithms: Isolation Forest, One-Class SVM, Autoencoders.

Example:

- Grouping customers based on purchasing behavior (clustering) or reducing the dimensions of a dataset for visualization (dimensionality reduction).

3. Reinforcement Learning (RL)

Reinforcement learning is a type of machine learning where an agent learns to make decisions by interacting with an environment. The agent receives feedback in the form of rewards or penalties based on its actions, and its goal is to maximize the cumulative reward over time.

Key Characteristics:

- Involves an agent, environment, actions, and rewards.
- The agent learns through trial and error.
- Commonly used in dynamic and interactive environments.

Examples of Reinforcement Learning Tasks:

- **Game Playing**: Training agents to play games like chess, Go, or video games (e.g., AlphaGo, OpenAI's Dota 2 bot).
- **Robotics**: Teaching robots to perform tasks like walking, grasping, or navigating.
- **Autonomous Systems**: Developing self-driving cars or drones.

Example:

- Training a robot to navigate a maze by rewarding it for reaching the goal and penalizing it for hitting obstacles.

Other Types of Machine Learning

In addition to the three main types, there are several other specialized categories of machine learning:

4. Semi-Supervised Learning

Semi-supervised learning combines a small amount of labeled data with a large amount of unlabeled data. It is useful when labeled data is expensive or difficult to obtain.

- **Example**: Using a small set of labeled images and a large set of unlabeled images to train an image classification model.

5. Self-Supervised Learning

Self-supervised learning is a form of unsupervised learning where the model generates its own labels from the input data. It is commonly used in representation learning.

- **Example**: Predicting missing parts of an image (inpainting) or predicting the next word in a sentence (language modeling).

6. Transfer Learning

Transfer learning involves leveraging knowledge learned from one task or domain and applying it to a different but related task or domain. It is particularly useful when labeled data is scarce.

- **Example**: Using a pre-trained image classification model (e.g., ResNet) and fine-tuning it for a specific task like medical image analysis.

7. Online Learning

Online learning involves training models incrementally as new data arrives, rather than training on the entire dataset at once. It is useful for applications where data arrives in a stream.

- **Example**: Updating a recommendation system in real-time as new user interactions occur.

8. Ensemble Learning

Ensemble learning combines multiple models to improve overall performance. It is based on the idea that a group of weak learners can collectively form a strong learner.

- **Example**: Random Forests (ensemble of decision trees) or Gradient Boosting Machines (GBM).

Type	Description	Examples
Supervised Learning	Learns from labeled data to predict outputs.	Classification, Regression.
Unsupervised Learning	Discovers patterns in unlabeled data.	Clustering, Dimensionality Reduction, Anomaly Detection.
Reinforcement Learning	Learns by interacting with an environment to maximize rewards.	Game Playing, Robotics, Autonomous Systems.
Semi-Supervised Learning	Combines a small amount of labeled data with a large amount of unlabeled data.	Image classification with limited labels.
Self-Supervised Learning	Generates labels from the data itself.	Image inpainting, Masked Language Modeling.
Transfer Learning	Transfers knowledge from one task/domain to another.	Fine-tuning pre-trained models for specific tasks.
Online Learning	Learns incrementally as new data arrives.	Real-time recommendation systems.
Ensemble Learning	Combines multiple models to improve performance.	Random Forests, Gradient Boosting Machines.

Summary of Machine Learning Types

## CHAPTER EIGHT

Supervised Learning

Supervised Machine Learning

Supervised machine learning is a type of machine learning where the model is trained on labeled data. The goal is to learn a mapping from input features to an output label, enabling the model to make predictions on new, unseen data. It is called "supervised" because the training process is guided by the labeled data, which acts as a teacher for the model.

Key Concepts in Supervised Learning

1. **Labeled Data:**

   - The dataset consists of input-output pairs, where the input is a set of features, and the output is the corresponding label (target variable).
   - Example: In a dataset for house price prediction, the features might include square footage, number of bedrooms, and location, while the label is the price of the house.

2. **Training:**

   - The model learns the relationship between the input features and the output label by minimizing a loss function (e.g., mean squared error for regression or cross-entropy for classification).

3. **Prediction:**

   - Once trained, the model can predict the output label for new, unseen input data.

4. **Evaluation:**

- The model's performance is evaluated using metrics like accuracy, precision, recall, F1-score (for classification), or mean squared error (for regression).

Types of Supervised Learning

1. **Classification**:

   - The goal is to predict a discrete label (category or class).
   - Examples:

     - Binary Classification: Two possible outcomes (e.g., spam or not spam).
     - Multiclass Classification: More than two possible outcomes (e.g., classifying images into cats, dogs, or birds).

2. **Regression**:

   - The goal is to predict a continuous value.
   - Examples:

     - Predicting house prices, stock prices, or temperature.

Steps in Supervised Learning

1. **Data Collection**:

   - Gather labeled data relevant to the problem.

2. **Data Preprocessing**:

   - Clean the data (handle missing values, outliers, etc.).
   - Normalize or standardize features.
   - Encode categorical variables.

3. **Feature Selection/Engineering**:

- Select relevant features or create new ones to improve model performance.

4. **Model Selection:**

   - Choose an appropriate algorithm (e.g., linear regression, decision trees, neural networks).

5. **Model Training:**

   - Train the model on the labeled dataset.

6. **Model Evaluation:**

   - Evaluate the model on a test dataset using appropriate metrics.

7. **Model Deployment:**

   - Deploy the trained model to make predictions on new data.

Algorithms in Supervised Learning

1. **Linear Regression:**

   - Used for regression tasks.
   - Predicts a continuous value based on a linear relationship between input features and the output.
   - Example: Predicting house prices based on square footage.

2. **Logistic Regression:**

   - Used for binary classification tasks.
   - Predicts the probability of an input belonging to a particular class.
   - Example: Predicting whether an email is spam or not.

3. **Decision Trees:**

   - Used for both classification and regression.

- Splits the data into branches based on feature values to make predictions.
- Example: Classifying whether a customer will buy a product based on age and income.

4. **Random Forests:**

   - An ensemble of decision trees.
   - Improves accuracy and reduces overfitting.
   - Example: Predicting loan default risk.

5. **Support Vector Machines (SVM):**

   - Used for classification and regression.
   - Finds the optimal hyperplane to separate data points into classes.
   - Example: Classifying images of handwritten digits.

6. **Neural Networks:**

   - Used for complex tasks like image recognition, natural language processing, etc.
   - Consists of layers of interconnected nodes (neurons).
   - Example: Classifying images of cats and dogs.

Examples of Supervised Learning

1. **Email Spam Detection:**

   - Input: Email text (features like word frequency, sender, subject).
   - Output: Label ("Spam" or "Not Spam").
   - Algorithm: Logistic regression, Naive Bayes, or SVM.

2. **House Price Prediction:**

   - Input: Features like square footage, number of bedrooms, location.
   - Output: Price of the house.
   - Algorithm: Linear regression, decision trees, or random forests.

3. **Medical Diagnosis:**

   - Input: Patient data (e.g., age, blood pressure, symptoms).
   - Output: Diagnosis (e.g., "Healthy" or "Diseased").
   - Algorithm: Logistic regression, decision trees, or neural networks.

4. **Image Classification:**

   - Input: Images of objects.
   - Output: Class label (e.g., "Cat," "Dog," "Car").
   - Algorithm: Convolutional Neural Networks (CNNs).

5. **Sentiment Analysis:**

   - Input: Text data (e.g., product reviews).
   - Output: Sentiment label (e.g., "Positive," "Negative," "Neutral").
   - Algorithm: Logistic regression, Naive Bayes, or recurrent neural networks (RNNs).

Advantages of Supervised Learning

- Clear feedback during training (via labeled data).
- High accuracy for well-defined problems.
- Wide range of applications (classification and regression).

Challenges of Supervised Learning

- Requires labeled data, which can be expensive and time-consuming to obtain.
- May overfit the training data if not regularized properly.
- Performance depends heavily on the quality and quantity of labeled data.

Real-World Applications of Supervised Learning

1. **Healthcare:**

   - Predicting disease outcomes based on patient data.
   - Example: Diagnosing diabetes using patient health records.

2. **Finance:**

    - Credit scoring and fraud detection.
    - Example: Predicting whether a loan applicant will default.

3. **Retail:**

    - Customer segmentation and recommendation systems.
    - Example: Recommending products based on purchase history.

4. **Natural Language Processing (NLP):**

    - Text classification and sentiment analysis.
    - Example: Classifying news articles into categories.

5. **Computer Vision:**

    - Object detection and facial recognition.
    - Example: Detecting pedestrians in self-driving car systems.

Conclusion

Supervised machine learning is a powerful approach for solving problems where labeled data is available. It is widely used in applications ranging from healthcare to finance and beyond. By understanding its concepts, algorithms, and applications, you can build models that make accurate predictions and drive decision-making. Let me know if you'd like to dive deeper into any specific algorithm or application!

## CHAPTER NINE

Unsupervised machine learning

Unsupervised machine learning is a type of machine learning where the model is trained on **unlabeled data**. Unlike supervised learning, there are no predefined labels or target variables. Instead, the goal is to discover hidden patterns, structures, or relationships within the data. Unsupervised learning is often used for exploratory data analysis, clustering, and dimensionality reduction.

Key Concepts in Unsupervised Learning

1. **Unlabeled Data:**

   - The dataset consists of input features without any corresponding output labels.
   - Example: A dataset of customer purchase histories without any predefined categories.

2. **Pattern Discovery:**

   - The model identifies inherent structures in the data, such as clusters, associations, or anomalies.

3. **No Guidance:**

   - Since there are no labels, the model learns purely from the input data without explicit feedback.

Types of Unsupervised Learning

1. **Clustering:**

   - Groups similar data points together based on their features.
   - Examples: Customer segmentation, image compression.

2. **Dimensionality Reduction:**

   - Reduces the number of features while preserving important information.
   - Examples: Visualizing high-dimensional data, improving computational efficiency.

3. **Association Rule Learning:**

   - Discovers relationships between variables in large datasets.
   - Examples: Market basket analysis, recommendation systems.

4. **Anomaly Detection:**

   - Identifies rare or unusual data points that deviate from the norm.
   - Examples: Fraud detection, network intrusion detection.

Steps in Unsupervised Learning

1. **Data Collection:**

   - Gather unlabeled data relevant to the problem.

2. **Data Preprocessing:**

   - Clean the data (handle missing values, outliers, etc.).
   - Normalize or standardize features.

3. **Feature Selection/Engineering:**

   - Select relevant features or create new ones to improve model performance.

4. **Model Selection:**

   - Choose an appropriate algorithm (e.g., K-means clustering, PCA).

5. **Model Training:**

   - Train the model on the unlabeled dataset.

6. **Evaluation:**

   - Evaluate the model using internal metrics (e.g., silhouette score for clustering).

7. **Interpretation:**

   - Analyze the results to gain insights or make decisions.

Algorithms in Unsupervised Learning

1. **K-Means Clustering:**

   - Groups data into K clusters based on similarity.
   - Example: Segmenting customers based on purchasing behavior.

2. **Hierarchical Clustering:**

   - Builds a tree-like structure of clusters.
   - Example: Organizing species into a taxonomy based on genetic data.

3. **Principal Component Analysis (PCA):**

   - Reduces the dimensionality of data while preserving variance.
   - Example: Visualizing high-dimensional data in 2D or 3D.

4. **t-Distributed Stochastic Neighbor Embedding (t-SNE):**

   - Reduces dimensionality for visualization.
   - Example: Visualizing clusters in high-dimensional data.

5. **Apriori Algorithm:**

   - Finds frequent itemsets and association rules.
   - Example: Market basket analysis (e.g., "Customers who buy bread also buy butter").

6. **DBSCAN (Density-Based Spatial Clustering of Applications with Noise):**

   - Identifies clusters of varying shapes and detects outliers.
   - Example: Detecting fraudulent transactions.

7. **Autoencoders:**

   - Neural networks used for dimensionality reduction and feature learning.
   - Example: Compressing images or detecting anomalies.

Examples of Unsupervised Learning

1. **Customer Segmentation:**

   - Input: Customer purchase history, demographics, and behavior.
   - Output: Groups of similar customers.
   - Algorithm: K-means clustering, hierarchical clustering.

2. **Image Compression:**

   - Input: High-resolution images.
   - Output: Compressed images with reduced file size.
   - Algorithm: K-means clustering (reduce the number of colors).

3. **Market Basket Analysis:**

   - Input: Transaction data from a retail store.
   - Output: Association rules (e.g., "Customers who buy chips also buy soda").
   - Algorithm: Apriori algorithm.

4. **Anomaly Detection**:

  - Input: Network traffic data.
  - Output: Identification of unusual patterns (e.g., cyberattacks).
  - Algorithm: DBSCAN, autoencoders.

5. **Topic Modeling**:

  - Input: Collection of text documents.
  - Output: Topics or themes in the documents.
  - Algorithm: Latent Dirichlet Allocation (LDA).

6. **Gene Clustering**:

  - Input: Gene expression data.
  - Output: Groups of genes with similar expression patterns.
  - Algorithm: Hierarchical clustering.

Advantages of Unsupervised Learning

- Does not require labeled data, which is often expensive and time-consuming to obtain.
- Useful for exploratory data analysis and discovering hidden patterns.
- Can handle complex, unstructured data (e.g., images, text).

Challenges of Unsupervised Learning

- Harder to evaluate model performance since there are no ground truth labels.
- Results can be subjective and require domain expertise to interpret.
- May produce less accurate results compared to supervised learning for specific tasks.

Real-World Applications of Unsupervised Learning

1. **Retail**:

  - Customer segmentation for targeted marketing.

- ◦ Example: Grouping customers based on purchasing behavior.

2. **Healthcare**:

   - ◦ Identifying patient groups with similar symptoms or conditions.
   - ◦ Example: Clustering patients for personalized treatment plans.

3. **Finance**:

   - ◦ Fraud detection by identifying unusual transaction patterns.
   - ◦ Example: Detecting credit card fraud.

4. **Natural Language Processing (NLP)**:

   - ◦ Topic modeling for document clustering.
   - ◦ Example: Organizing news articles into categories.

5. **Computer Vision**:

   - ◦ Image segmentation and object recognition.
   - ◦ Example: Identifying objects in satellite images.

6. **Social Network Analysis**:

   - ◦ Community detection in social networks.
   - ◦ Example: Identifying groups of users with similar interests.

## CHAPTER TEN

Self-Supervised Machine Learning

Self-supervised learning (SSL) is a paradigm in machine learning where models are trained to learn meaningful representations of data without requiring explicit human-labeled annotations. Instead of relying on labeled datasets, SSL leverages the inherent structure or relationships within the data itself to generate supervisory signals. This approach is particularly useful in scenarios where labeled data is scarce, expensive, or time-consuming to obtain.

SSL has gained significant attention in recent years due to its ability to leverage large amounts of unlabeled data, which is often more readily available than labeled data. It has been successfully applied in various domains, including computer vision, natural language processing (NLP), and speech recognition.

How Self-Supervised Learning Works

The core idea of SSL is to design a **pretext task** that allows the model to learn useful representations of the data. The pretext task is a surrogate task that is automatically generated from the data itself. Once the model learns these representations, they can be transferred to downstream tasks (e.g., classification, detection, or segmentation) with minimal fine-tuning.

The general workflow of SSL involves:

1. **Pretext Task Design**: Create a task that can be solved using the unlabeled data. The task should encourage the model to learn features that are useful for downstream tasks.
2. **Representation Learning**: Train the model on the pretext task to learn meaningful representations.

3. **Transfer Learning**: Use the learned representations for downstream tasks, often with a small amount of labeled data.

Examples of Self-Supervised Learning
1. Computer Vision
In computer vision, SSL has been widely used to learn visual representations from unlabeled images. Some common pretext tasks include:

- **Image Inpainting**: The model is trained to predict missing parts of an image. For example, a portion of the image is masked, and the model learns to reconstruct the missing pixels.
- **Rotation Prediction**: Images are rotated by a certain degree (e.g., 0°, 90°, 180°, 270°), and the model is trained to predict the rotation angle. This encourages the model to understand the spatial structure of objects.
- **Jigsaw Puzzles**: An image is divided into patches, and the model is trained to rearrange the patches into the correct order.
- **Contrastive Learning**: Methods like SimCLR, MoCo, and BYOL train models to maximize the similarity between different augmented views of the same image while minimizing the similarity between views of different images.

Example: SimCLR (Simple Framework for Contrastive Learning of Representations) uses data augmentation (e.g., cropping, color distortion) to create multiple views of the same image. The model is trained to bring the representations of these views closer in the feature space while pushing apart representations of different images.
2. Natural Language Processing (NLP)
In NLP, SSL has been instrumental in learning language representations from large text corpora. Some common pretext tasks include:

- **Masked Language Modeling (MLM)**: Popularized by BERT (Bidirectional Encoder Representations from Transformers), this task involves masking certain words in a sentence and training the model to predict the masked words based on the surrounding context.
- **Next Sentence Prediction (NSP)**: The model is trained to predict whether one sentence follows another in a document. This helps the model understand relationships between sentences.

- **Contrastive Learning**: Methods like SimCSE (Simple Contrastive Learning of Sentence Embeddings) train models to bring the representations of semantically similar sentences closer together while pushing apart dissimilar ones.

Example: BERT uses MLM and NSP as pretext tasks to learn contextualized word embeddings. These embeddings can then be fine-tuned for tasks like sentiment analysis, question answering, and named entity recognition.

3. Speech and Audio Processing

In speech recognition and audio processing, SSL has been used to learn representations from unlabeled audio data. Some common pretext tasks include:

- **Masked Acoustic Modeling**: Similar to MLM in NLP, parts of the audio signal are masked, and the model is trained to predict the missing segments.
- **Contrastive Predictive Coding (CPC)**: The model is trained to predict future segments of the audio signal based on past segments, encouraging it to learn meaningful representations of the audio.

Example: Wav2Vec 2.0 is a self-supervised model that learns speech representations by predicting masked segments of raw audio. These representations can then be fine-tuned for tasks like speech recognition.

4. Reinforcement Learning

In reinforcement learning (RL), SSL can be used to learn representations of the environment without explicit rewards. For example:

- **State Prediction**: The model is trained to predict the next state of the environment given the current state and action.
- **Time-Contrastive Learning**: The model learns to distinguish between states that are close in time and those that are far apart.

Example: In robotics, SSL can be used to learn representations of the environment that are useful for tasks like navigation or object manipulation.

Advantages of Self-Supervised Learning

1. **Reduced Dependency on Labeled Data**: SSL can leverage vast amounts of unlabeled data, which is often easier and cheaper to collect than labeled data.
2. **Transferability**: Representations learned through SSL can be transferred to multiple downstream tasks, reducing the need for task-specific training.
3. **Scalability**: SSL can scale to large datasets and complex models, making it suitable for modern deep learning architectures.

Challenges in Self-Supervised Learning

1. **Pretext Task Design**: Designing effective pretext tasks that lead to useful representations can be challenging and domain-specific.
2. **Evaluation**: Evaluating the quality of learned representations without downstream tasks can be difficult.
3. **Computational Cost**: Training SSL models often requires significant computational resources, especially for large datasets.

Conclusion

Self-supervised learning is a powerful paradigm that enables machines to learn meaningful representations from unlabeled data. By designing clever pretext tasks, SSL has achieved state-of-the-art results in various domains, including computer vision, NLP, and speech processing. As research in SSL continues to advance, it holds the potential to further reduce the reliance on labeled data and unlock new possibilities in artificial intelligence

## CHAPTER ELEVEN

Transfer learning

Transfer learning is a machine learning technique where a model developed for one task is reused as the starting point for a model on a second task. This approach is particularly useful when the second task has limited data, as it allows the model to leverage knowledge learned from the first task, which is typically data-rich. Transfer learning is widely used in various domains, including computer vision, natural language processing (NLP), and speech recognition.

How Transfer Learning Works

1. **Pre-trained Models**: A model is first trained on a large, general dataset (e.g., ImageNet for images or Wikipedia for text). This model learns general features that are useful for a wide range of tasks.
2. **Fine-tuning**: The pre-trained model is then fine-tuned on a smaller, task-specific dataset. During fine-tuning, the model adjusts its parameters to better fit the new task while retaining the general knowledge from the pre-training phase.

Benefits of Transfer Learning

- **Reduced Training Time**: Since the model starts with pre-trained weights, it requires less time to converge on the new task.
- **Improved Performance**: Transfer learning often leads to better performance, especially when the target dataset is small.
- **Resource Efficiency**: It reduces the need for large amounts of labeled data and computational resources.

Examples of Transfer Learning

1. Computer Vision

- **Image Classification**: A model pre-trained on ImageNet (a large dataset of labeled images) can be fine-tuned to classify specific types of images, such as medical images (e.g., X-rays or MRIs). For example, a model trained to recognize general objects can be adapted to detect tumors in medical scans.
- **Object Detection**: Models like YOLO (You Only Look Once) or Faster R-CNN, pre-trained on large datasets, can be fine-tuned for specific object detection tasks, such as detecting pedestrians in autonomous driving systems.

2. Natural Language Processing (NLP)

- **Sentiment Analysis**: Pre-trained language models like BERT (Bidirectional Encoder Representations from Transformers) or GPT (Generative Pre-trained Transformer) can be fine-tuned to analyze sentiment in product reviews or social media posts. For instance, a model trained on a large corpus of text can be adapted to determine whether a tweet expresses positive or negative sentiment.
- **Machine Translation**: Models like Google's Transformer, pre-trained on large multilingual corpora, can be fine-tuned for specific language pairs, such as translating between English and French.

3. Speech Recognition

- **Voice Assistants**: Models pre-trained on large datasets of spoken language can be fine-tuned for specific tasks, such as recognizing commands for voice assistants like Siri or Alexa. For example, a model trained on general speech data can be adapted to understand specific accents or dialects.
- **Speech-to-Text**: Pre-trained models like Wav2Vec can be fine-tuned to transcribe audio recordings in specific domains, such as medical dictations or legal proceedings.

4. Healthcare

- **Disease Diagnosis**: Models pre-trained on general medical imaging datasets can be fine-tuned to diagnose specific diseases, such as pneumonia from chest X-rays or skin cancer from dermatology images.
- **Drug Discovery**: Pre-trained models on chemical compound datasets can be fine-tuned to predict the efficacy of new drugs or identify potential side effects.

5. Autonomous Vehicles

- **Scene Understanding**: Models pre-trained on large datasets of urban scenes can be fine-tuned to understand specific driving environments, such as recognizing traffic signs, pedestrians, or other vehicles in real-time.
- **Path Planning**: Pre-trained models can be adapted to predict the best routes or maneuvers for autonomous vehicles based on real-time sensor data.

Challenges and Considerations

- **Domain Mismatch**: The pre-trained model may not always align well with the target task, leading to suboptimal performance. Careful selection of the pre-trained model and fine-tuning strategy is crucial.
- **Overfitting**: When fine-tuning on a small dataset, there's a risk of overfitting. Techniques like regularization, data augmentation, and early stopping can help mitigate this.

Computational Resources: While transfer learning reduces the need for large datasets, fine-tuning still requires significant computational resources, especially for large models

## CHAPTER TWELVE

Reinforcement Learning

Reinforcement Learning (RL) is a type of machine learning where an agent learns to make decisions by performing actions in an environment to maximize some notion of cumulative reward. Unlike supervised learning, where the model is trained on a labeled dataset, RL involves learning from interactions with the environment through trial and error. This makes RL particularly well-suited for problems where the optimal solution is not known in advance but can be discovered through exploration.

Key Concepts in Reinforcement Learning

1. **Agent**: The learner or decision-maker.
2. **Environment**: The world in which the agent operates.
3. **State (s)**: A representation of the current situation of the agent.
4. **Action (a)**: A move or decision made by the agent.
5. **Reward (r)**: Feedback from the environment based on the action taken.
6. **Policy (π)**: A strategy that the agent employs to determine the next action based on the current state.
7. **Value Function (V)**: A prediction of future rewards, used to evaluate the goodness of a state.
8. **Q-Value (Q)**: The expected cumulative reward for taking a particular action in a particular state and following the policy thereafter.

How Reinforcement Learning Works

1. **Initialization**: The agent starts in an initial state.
2. **Interaction**: The agent takes an action based on its policy.
3. **Feedback**: The environment provides a reward and transitions to a new state.

4. **Learning**: The agent updates its policy based on the reward received and the new state.
5. **Iteration**: The process repeats until the agent learns an optimal policy that maximizes cumulative rewards.

Examples of Reinforcement Learning

1. **Game Playing**

   - **AlphaGo**: Developed by DeepMind, AlphaGo is an RL-based system that defeated the world champion in the game of Go. The agent learned by playing millions of games against itself, improving its policy over time.
   - **Chess and Shogi**: AlphaZero, another DeepMind project, used RL to master chess and shogi by playing against itself and learning from the outcomes.

2. **Robotics**

   - **Autonomous Robots**: RL is used to train robots to perform complex tasks such as walking, grasping objects, or assembling parts. For example, a robot arm can learn to pick and place objects by receiving rewards for successful actions.
   - **Drone Navigation**: Drones can use RL to learn how to navigate through obstacles and reach a target destination efficiently.

3. **Autonomous Vehicles**

   - **Self-Driving Cars**: RL algorithms help autonomous vehicles learn driving policies by simulating various driving scenarios. The agent receives rewards for safe and efficient driving and penalties for collisions or traffic violations.
   - **Traffic Light Control**: RL can optimize traffic light timings to reduce congestion and improve traffic flow in urban areas.

4. **Healthcare**

- ◦ **Personalized Treatment Plans**: RL can be used to develop personalized treatment plans for patients by learning optimal dosages and treatment schedules based on patient responses.
- ◦ **Medical Diagnosis**: RL algorithms can assist in diagnosing diseases by learning from historical patient data and outcomes.

5. Finance

- ◦ **Algorithmic Trading**: RL is used to develop trading strategies that maximize returns by learning from market data and past trades.
- ◦ **Portfolio Management**: RL can optimize asset allocation in a portfolio by learning to balance risk and return based on market conditions.

6. Recommendation Systems

- ◦ **Personalized Recommendations**: RL can improve recommendation systems by learning user preferences over time and suggesting content that maximizes user engagement and satisfaction.
- ◦ **Dynamic Pricing**: E-commerce platforms use RL to adjust prices dynamically based on demand, competition, and user behavior to maximize revenue.

7. Natural Language Processing (NLP)

- ◦ **Dialogue Systems**: RL is used to train chatbots and virtual assistants to engage in more natural and effective conversations by learning from user interactions.
- ◦ **Text Summarization**: RL can optimize summarization models to produce concise and informative summaries by rewarding coherence and relevance.

Challenges and Considerations

- **Exploration vs. Exploitation**: The agent must balance exploring new actions to discover their effects and exploiting known actions that yield high rewards.

- **Sparse Rewards**: In some environments, rewards are sparse, making it difficult for the agent to learn effectively. Techniques like reward shaping can help.
- **Scalability**: RL can be computationally expensive, especially in environments with large state and action spaces. Advanced algorithms and hardware acceleration are often required.
- **Safety and Ethics**: Ensuring that RL agents behave safely and ethically, especially in critical applications like healthcare and autonomous driving, is crucial.

Conclusion

Reinforcement Learning is a powerful paradigm for training agents to make sequential decisions in complex environments. Its applications span a wide range of domains, from game playing and robotics to healthcare and finance. By learning through interaction and feedback, RL agents can discover optimal policies that maximize long-term rewards, making it a key technology in the advancement of artificial intelligence. However, challenges such as exploration-exploitation trade-offs, sparse rewards, and scalability must be addressed to fully realize its potential.

## CHAPTER THIRTEEN

Ensemble Machine Learning

Ensemble machine learning is a powerful technique that combines the predictions of multiple individual models to improve overall performance. The core idea behind ensemble methods is that a group of weak learners (models that perform slightly better than random guessing) can be combined to create a strong learner (a model with significantly better performance). This approach often leads to more accurate, robust, and generalizable predictions compared to using a single model.

Key Concepts in Ensemble Learning

Diversity of Models:

Ensemble methods rely on the diversity of the individual models. If all models make the same errors, combining them will not improve performance. Diversity can be achieved by using different algorithms, training on different subsets of data, or using different features.

Bias-Variance Tradeoff:

Ensemble methods help balance the bias-variance tradeoff. For example, bagging reduces variance, while boosting reduces bias. This leads to better generalization on unseen data.

Types of Ensemble Methods:

There are several popular ensemble techniques, each with its own approach to combining models:

Bagging (Bootstrap Aggregating): Trains multiple models independently on different subsets of the training data (sampled with replacement) and averages their predictions. Example: Random Forest.

Boosting: Trains models sequentially, where each new model focuses on correcting the errors of the previous ones. Example: AdaBoost, Gradient Boosting Machines (GBM), and XGBoost.

Stacking: Combines the predictions of multiple models using a meta-model (also called a blender or meta-learner) to produce the final output.

Voting: Combines predictions from multiple models by majority voting (for classification) or averaging (for regression).

Advantages of Ensemble Learning

Improved Accuracy:

By combining multiple models, ensemble methods often achieve higher accuracy than any single model.

Robustness:

Ensembles are less prone to overfitting and more robust to noise in the data.

Versatility:

Ensemble methods can be applied to a wide range of machine learning tasks, including classification, regression, and anomaly detection.

Handling Complex Relationships:

Ensembles can capture complex patterns in the data that might be missed by individual models.

Popular Ensemble Algorithms

Random Forest:

A bagging-based ensemble method that uses decision trees as base learners. It introduces randomness by selecting a subset of features for each split, reducing overfitting and improving generalization.

Gradient Boosting Machines (GBM):

A boosting-based method that builds models sequentially, with each new model minimizing the errors of the previous ones using gradient descent.

XGBoost:

An optimized implementation of gradient boosting that is highly efficient and scalable, often used in competitions and real-world applications.

AdaBoost:

A boosting algorithm that focuses on misclassified samples by assigning higher weights to them in subsequent iterations.

Stacking:

Combines predictions from multiple models using a meta-model, such as logistic regression or a neural network, to produce the final output.

Challenges and Considerations

Computational Complexity:

Ensemble methods can be computationally expensive, as they require training and maintaining multiple models.

Interpretability:

Ensembles, especially complex ones like boosting or stacking, can be harder to interpret compared to single models.

Overfitting Risk:

While ensembles are generally robust, certain methods (e.g., boosting) can overfit if not properly regularized.

Hyperparameter Tuning:

Ensemble methods often have multiple hyperparameters that need to be carefully tuned for optimal performance.

Applications of Ensemble Learning

Competitions:

Ensemble methods are widely used in machine learning competitions (e.g., Kaggle) to achieve top rankings.

Finance:

Used for credit scoring, fraud detection, and stock price prediction.

Healthcare:

Applied in disease diagnosis, patient outcome prediction, and medical image analysis.

Natural Language Processing (NLP):

Used for sentiment analysis, text classification, and machine translation.

Computer Vision:

Applied in object detection, image classification, and facial recognition.

Conclusion

Ensemble machine learning is a versatile and powerful approach that leverages the strengths of multiple models to achieve superior performance. By combining diverse models, ensemble methods address the limitations of individual learners and provide robust, accurate, and generalizable solutions. While they come with challenges such as computational complexity and interpretability, their benefits often outweigh these drawbacks, making them a popular choice in both research and industry. As machine learning continues to evolve, ensemble methods will remain a key tool in the data scientist's toolkit.

## CHAPTER FOURTEEN

Choosing the Right Algorithm

Choosing the right machine learning algorithm for a given problem depends on several factors, including the nature of the problem, the characteristics of the data, and the desired outcome. Here's a structured approach to help you decide:

1. Understand the Problem Type

- **Supervised Learning:**

  - **Classification**: Predicting a categorical label (e.g., spam detection, image classification).

    - Algorithms: Logistic Regression, Decision Trees, Random Forest, SVM, k-Nearest Neighbors (k-NN), Neural Networks.

  - **Regression**: Predicting a continuous value (e.g., house price prediction, stock price forecasting).

    - Algorithms: Linear Regression, Decision Trees, Random Forest, Gradient Boosting, Neural Networks.

- **Unsupervised Learning:**

  - **Clustering**: Grouping similar data points (e.g., customer segmentation, anomaly detection).

    - Algorithms: k-Means, Hierarchical Clustering, DBSCAN, Gaussian Mixture Models.

- ◦ **Dimensionality Reduction**: Reducing the number of features (e.g., visualization, feature extraction).

    - ▪ Algorithms: PCA, t-SNE, UMAP.

- **Reinforcement Learning**:

  - ◦ Learning through interaction with an environment (e.g., game playing, robotics).

    - ▪ Algorithms: Q-Learning, Deep Q-Networks (DQN), Policy Gradient Methods.

2. Analyze the Data

- **Size of the Dataset**:

  - ◦ Small datasets: Use simpler models (e.g., Linear Regression, Logistic Regression) to avoid overfitting.
  - ◦ Large datasets: Use scalable algorithms (e.g., Random Forest, Gradient Boosting, Neural Networks).

- **Dimensionality**:

  - ◦ High-dimensional data: Use algorithms that handle dimensionality well (e.g., PCA, SVM, Neural Networks).
  - ◦ Low-dimensional data: Simpler algorithms (e.g., k-NN, Decision Trees) may suffice.

- **Data Quality**:

  - ◦ Missing data: Use algorithms that handle missing data (e.g., Random Forest, XGBoost) or preprocess the data.
  - ◦ Noisy data: Use robust algorithms (e.g., SVM, Ensemble Methods).

- **Feature Types**:

  - ◦ Numerical features: Most algorithms work well.

- ○ Categorical features: Use algorithms that handle categorical data (e.g., Decision Trees, Random Forest) or encode them (e.g., one-hot encoding).

3. Consider Model Complexity

- **Interpretability:**

  - ○ If interpretability is important, use simpler models (e.g., Linear Regression, Decision Trees).
  - ○ If interpretability is not critical, use complex models (e.g., Neural Networks, Ensemble Methods).

- **Training Time:**

  - ○ For quick training, use simpler models (e.g., Logistic Regression, k-NN).
  - ○ For better performance, use more complex models (e.g., Random Forest, Neural Networks), but be prepared for longer training times.

4. Evaluate Performance Metrics

- **Classification:**

  - ○ Accuracy, Precision, Recall, F1-Score, ROC-AUC.

- **Regression:**

  - ○ Mean Squared Error (MSE), Mean Absolute Error (MAE), R^2.

- **Clustering:**

  - ○ Silhouette Score, Davies-Bouldin Index.

Choose an algorithm that optimizes the relevant metric for your problem.

5. Experiment and Compare

- Start with a baseline model (e.g., Linear Regression for regression, Logistic Regression for classification).
- Experiment with multiple algorithms and compare their performance using cross-validation.
- Use techniques like hyperparameter tuning to optimize the chosen algorithm.

6. Consider Domain-Specific Requirements

- **Real-Time Predictions:**

  - Use fast algorithms (e.g., Logistic Regression, Decision Trees).

- **Scalability:**

  - Use scalable algorithms (e.g., Random Forest, Gradient Boosting, Neural Networks).

- **Resource Constraints:**

  - Use lightweight algorithms (e.g., k-NN, Decision Trees) if computational resources are limited.

Problem Type	Algorithm
Classification	Logistic Regression, Decision Trees, Random Forest, SVM, k-NN, Neural Networks
Regression	Linear Regression, Decision Trees, Random Forest, Gradient Boosting, Neural Networks
Clustering	k-Means, Hierarchical Clustering, DBSCAN, Gaussian Mixture Models
Dimensionality Reduction	PCA, t-SNE, UMAP
Anomaly Detection	Isolation Forest, One-Class SVM, Autoencoders
Time Series	ARIMA, LSTM, Prophet

Algorithm Selection Cheat Sheet

Example Workflow

1. **Problem**: Predict whether a customer will churn (binary classification).
2. **Data**: 10,000 rows, 20 features (mix of numerical and categorical).
3. **Steps**:

   - Preprocess data (handle missing values, encode categorical features).
   - Start with Logistic Regression as a baseline.
   - Experiment with Random Forest, Gradient Boosting, and SVM.
   - Compare performance using ROC-AUC and F1-Score.
   - Select the best-performing model and tune hyperparameters.

Summary

- **Understand the problem type** (classification, regression, clustering, etc.).
- **Analyze the data** (size, dimensionality, quality, feature types).
- **Consider model complexity** (interpretability, training time).
- **Evaluate performance metrics** relevant to the problem.
- **Experiment and compare** multiple algorithms.
- **Consider domain-specific requirements** (real-time predictions, scalability, resource constraints).

By following this structured approach, you can systematically choose the most appropriate machine learning algorithm for your problem.

## CHAPTER FIFTEEN

Overfitting and Underfitting

In machine learning, **overfitting** and **underfitting** are two common problems that occur when training a model. Both issues arise due to the model's inability to generalize well to unseen data, but they stem from opposite causes. Understanding these concepts is crucial for building effective and robust machine learning models.

1. Overfitting

Overfitting occurs when a model learns the training data **too well**, capturing not only the underlying patterns but also the noise and outliers. As a result, the model performs exceptionally well on the training data but fails to generalize to new, unseen data.

Characteristics of Overfitting:

- High accuracy on the training dataset.
- Poor performance on the validation or test dataset.
- The model is overly complex, with too many parameters relative to the amount of training data.
- The model captures noise and irrelevant details in the training data.

Causes of Overfitting:

- Using a model that is too complex (e.g., a deep neural network with too many layers or a decision tree with excessive depth).
- Training for too many epochs (common in deep learning).
- Insufficient training data relative to the model's complexity.
- Not using regularization techniques.

How to Prevent Overfitting:

- **Regularization:** Techniques like L1 (Lasso) or L2 (Ridge) regularization penalize large coefficients, discouraging overly complex models.
- **Cross-validation:** Use techniques like k-fold cross-validation to evaluate the model's performance on multiple subsets of the data.
- **Early stopping:** In iterative algorithms like gradient descent, stop training when performance on the validation set starts to degrade.
- **Simplify the model:** Reduce the number of features or use a less complex model architecture.
- **Data augmentation:** Increase the size and diversity of the training dataset.
- **Dropout:** In neural networks, randomly drop units during training to prevent over-reliance on specific neurons.

2. Underfitting

Underfitting occurs when a model is **too simple** to capture the underlying patterns in the data. As a result, the model performs poorly on both the training data and unseen data.

Characteristics of Underfitting:

- Low accuracy on both the training and test datasets.
- The model is too simplistic, failing to capture the complexity of the data.
- High bias and low variance.

Causes of Underfitting:

- Using a model that is too simple (e.g., linear regression for a non-linear problem).
- Insufficient training time or epochs.
- Not using enough features or failing to engineer meaningful features.
- Over-regularization, which constrains the model too much.

How to Prevent Underfitting:

- **Increase model complexity:** Use a more sophisticated model (e.g., switch from linear regression to a polynomial regression or a decision tree).
- **Feature engineering:** Add more relevant features or create new features that better represent the data.

- **Reduce regularization:** Decrease the strength of regularization techniques.
- **Train longer:** Allow the model to train for more epochs or iterations.
- **Ensemble methods:** Combine multiple models to improve performance.

3. The Bias-Variance Tradeoff

Overfitting and underfitting are closely related to the **bias-variance tradeoff**, a fundamental concept in machine learning:

- **Bias:** Error due to overly simplistic assumptions in the model. High bias leads to underfitting.
- **Variance:** Error due to the model's sensitivity to small fluctuations in the training set. High variance leads to overfitting.

The goal is to find a balance where the model has **low bias** and **low variance**, ensuring it generalizes well to new data.

4. Visualizing Overfitting and Underfitting

- **Underfitting:** The model's curve (e.g., a straight line in regression) does not fit the data well, missing key trends.
- **Overfitting:** The model's curve fits the training data perfectly, including noise, resulting in a jagged or overly complex shape.
- **Good Fit:** The model captures the underlying trend without being overly complex or too simplistic.

5. Practical Tips to Avoid Overfitting and Underfitting

1. **Start with a simple model:** Begin with a basic model and gradually increase complexity if needed.
2. **Use validation data:** Always evaluate the model on a separate validation set to monitor performance.
3. **Regularization:** Apply regularization techniques to control model complexity.
4. **Feature selection:** Use only relevant features to avoid unnecessary complexity.
5. **Hyperparameter tuning:** Optimize hyperparameters using techniques like grid search or random search.

6. **Ensemble methods:** Use methods like bagging (e.g., Random Forests) or boosting (e.g., Gradient Boosting) to improve generalization.

## CHAPTER SIXTEEN

Data Representation in Machine Learning

Data representation is a fundamental concept in machine learning (ML) that refers to how data is structured and formatted for use in ML algorithms. The way data is represented can significantly impact the performance and accuracy of a model. Below is a detailed explanation of data representation in machine learning, including types of data, feature engineering, and common techniques for representing data.

1. Types of Data in Machine Learning

a) Structured Data

- Definition: Data organized in a tabular format (rows and columns).
- Examples:

  - CSV files.
  - SQL databases.
  - Excel spreadsheets.

- Use Cases: Regression, classification, and clustering.

b) Unstructured Data

- Definition: Data without a predefined structure.
- Examples:

  - Text (e.g., emails, articles).
  - Images.
  - Audio and video.

- Use Cases: Natural language processing (NLP), computer vision, and speech recognition.

c) Semi-Structured Data

- Definition: Data that does not conform to a strict schema but has some organizational properties.
- Examples:

  - JSON files.
  - XML files.

- Use Cases: Web scraping, APIs, and data integration.

2. Feature Representation
a) Numerical Data

- Definition: Data represented as numbers.
- Types:

  - Continuous: Values within a range (e.g., temperature, age).
  - Discrete: Integer values (e.g., number of children).

- Representation:

  - Directly used as input to ML models.
  - May require scaling (e.g., normalization, standardization).

b) Categorical Data

- Definition: Data representing categories or labels.
- Types:

  - Nominal: No inherent order (e.g., colors, countries).
  - Ordinal: Ordered categories (e.g., ratings, education levels).

- Representation:

- ○ One-Hot Encoding: Converts categories into binary vectors.

```python
Copy
# Example: One-hot encoding
import pandas as pd
data = pd.DataFrame({'color': ['red', 'blue', 'green']})
encoded_data = pd.get_dummies(data)
```

- ○ Label Encoding: Assigns a unique integer to each category.

```python
Copy
# Example: Label encoding
from sklearn.preprocessing import LabelEncoder
encoder = LabelEncoder()
data['color_encoded'] = encoder.fit_transform(data['color'])
c) Text Data
```

- Definition: Data in the form of text.
- Representation:

- ○ Bag of Words (BoW): Represents text as a vector of word frequencies.

```python
Copy
# Example: Bag of Words
from sklearn.feature_extraction.text import CountVectorizer
vectorizer = CountVectorizer()
X = vectorizer.fit_transform(['I love machine learning', 'Machine learning is fun'])
```

- ○ TF-IDF: Represents text based on word importance.

```python
Copy
# Example: TF-IDF
from sklearn.feature_extraction.text import TfidfVectorizer
```

vectorizer = TfidfVectorizer()
X = vectorizer.fit_transform(['I love machine learning', 'Machine learning is fun'])

- Word Embeddings: Represents words as dense vectors (e.g., Word2Vec, GloVe).

d) Image Data

- Definition: Data in the form of images.
- Representation:

  - Pixel Values: Images are represented as matrices of pixel values.
  - Preprocessing:

    - Resizing.
    - Normalization (e.g., scaling pixel values to [0, 1]).
    - Data augmentation (e.g., rotation, flipping).

e) Time Series Data

- Definition: Data collected over time.
- Representation:

  - Sequence Format: Represented as a sequence of values.
  - Preprocessing:

    - Resampling.
    - Feature engineering (e.g., rolling averages, lag features).

3. Feature Engineering
a) Feature Scaling

- Purpose: Normalize or standardize numerical features to ensure equal contribution to the model.
- Techniques:

  - Normalization: Scales values to a range (e.g., [0, 1]).

```python
python
Copy
from sklearn.preprocessing import MinMaxScaler
scaler = MinMaxScaler()
X_scaled = scaler.fit_transform(X)
```

- Standardization: Scales values to have a mean of 0 and a standard deviation of 1.

```python
python
Copy
from sklearn.preprocessing import StandardScaler
scaler = StandardScaler()
X_scaled = scaler.fit_transform(X)
```

b) Feature Extraction

- Purpose: Reduce dimensionality by creating new features from existing ones.
- Techniques:

  - Principal Component Analysis (PCA): Reduces dimensionality while preserving variance.

```python
python
Copy
from sklearn.decomposition import PCA
pca = PCA(n_components=2)
X_pca = pca.fit_transform(X)
```

  - Feature Selection: Selects the most relevant features (e.g., using correlation, mutual information).

c) Handling Missing Data

- Techniques:

  - Imputation: Fill missing values with mean, median, or mode.

```python
Copy
from sklearn.impute import SimpleImputer
imputer = SimpleImputer(strategy='mean')
X_imputed = imputer.fit_transform(X)
```

- ◦ Deletion: Remove rows or columns with missing values.

4. Common Data Representation Techniques
a) Vectorization

- Definition: Converting data into numerical vectors for ML models.
- Examples:

  - ◦ Text to word vectors.
  - ◦ Images to pixel vectors.

b) Embeddings

- Definition: Representing data in a lower-dimensional space while preserving relationships.
- Examples:

  - ◦ Word embeddings (e.g., Word2Vec, GloVe).
  - ◦ Graph embeddings (e.g., node2vec).

c) Graphs

- Definition: Representing data as nodes and edges.
- Use Cases:

  - ◦ Social network analysis.
  - ◦ Recommendation systems.

5. Tools for Data Representation
a) Python Libraries

- NumPy: For numerical data manipulation.

- Pandas: For structured data manipulation.
- Scikit-learn: For feature engineering and preprocessing.
- TensorFlow/PyTorch: For deep learning and advanced data representations.

b) Visualization Tools

- Matplotlib/Seaborn: For data visualization.
- Tableau/Power BI: For interactive data exploration.

6. Best Practices for Data Representation

1. Understand the Data: Analyze the data distribution and relationships.
2. Handle Missing Values: Use imputation or deletion techniques.
3. Normalize/Standardize Data: Ensure features are on a similar scale.
4. Encode Categorical Data: Use one-hot encoding or label encoding.
5. Reduce Dimensionality: Use PCA or feature selection to avoid overfitting.
6. Visualize Data: Use plots to identify patterns and outliers.

By understanding and applying these data representation techniques, you can prepare high-quality data for machine learning models, leading to better performance and more accurate predictions.

## CHAPTER SEVENTEEN

The Cost Function

The **cost function** (also known as a **loss function** or **objective function**) is a fundamental concept in machine learning. It quantifies how well a machine learning model is performing by measuring the difference between the model's predictions and the actual target values. The purpose of the cost function is to guide the learning process by providing a metric that the model aims to minimize during training.

Purpose of a Cost Function

1. **Measure Model Performance:**

   - The cost function evaluates how far the model's predictions are from the true values.
   - It provides a single scalar value that represents the "cost" or "error" of the model's predictions.

2. **Guide Model Optimization:**

   - During training, the model adjusts its parameters (e.g., weights in a neural network) to minimize the cost function.
   - Optimization algorithms like gradient descent use the cost function to determine the direction and magnitude of parameter updates.

3. **Act as a Feedback Mechanism:**

   - The cost function provides feedback to the model about its performance, enabling it to learn and improve over time.

4. **Enable Comparison of Models:**

- ◦ Different models or configurations can be compared based on their cost function values.
- ◦ A lower cost indicates better performance.

Key Properties of a Cost Function

1. **Differentiable:**

   - ◦ The cost function must be differentiable so that optimization algorithms like gradient descent can compute gradients and update model parameters.

2. **Convex (for some models):**

   - ◦ For simpler models like linear regression, a convex cost function ensures that there is a single global minimum, making optimization easier.

3. **Represents the Problem:**

   - ◦ The cost function should align with the problem being solved. For example, mean squared error is suitable for regression, while cross-entropy loss is better for classification.

Common Cost Functions in Machine Learning
1. Mean Squared Error (MSE):

- Used for **regression** problems.
- Measures the average squared difference between predicted and actual values.

2. Mean Absolute Error (MAE):

- Used for **regression** problems.
- Measures the average absolute difference between predicted and actual values.

3. Cross-Entropy Loss (Log Loss):

- Used for **classification** problems.
- Measures the performance of a classification model whose output is a probability value (between 0 and 1).

4. Hinge Loss:

- Used for **support vector machines (SVMs)** and binary classification.
- Penalizes predictions that are on the wrong side of the decision boundary..

5. Categorical Cross-Entropy Loss:

- Used for **multi-class classification** problems.
- Measures the difference between the predicted probability distribution and the true distribution.

How the Cost Function Works in Model Training

1. **Initialization:**

   ◦ The model starts with random or predefined parameters.

2. **Prediction:**

   ◦ The model makes predictions based on the current parameters.

3. **Cost Calculation:**

   ◦ The cost function computes the error between the predictions and the actual values.

4. **Optimization:**

   ◦ The model updates its parameters using optimization algorithms (e.g., gradient descent) to minimize the cost function.

5. **Iteration:**

- Steps 2-4 are repeated until the cost function converges to a minimum or a stopping criterion is met.

Why is the Cost Function Important?

1. **Drives Learning:**

   - The cost function is the foundation of the learning process. Without it, the model would not know how to adjust its parameters to improve performance.

2. **Ensures Generalization:**

   - By minimizing the cost function, the model learns to make predictions that generalize well to unseen data.

3. **Tailored to Problem Type:**

   - Different cost functions are designed for different types of problems (e.g., regression vs. classification), ensuring that the model is optimized for the task at hand.

4. **Enables Comparison:**

   - The cost function provides a quantitative measure to compare different models or hyperparameter settings.

## CHAPTER EIGHTEEN

Handling Missing Data

Handling missing data is a critical step in data preprocessing, as most machine learning algorithms cannot handle incomplete datasets directly. The approach to handling missing data depends on the nature of the data, the amount of missing values, and the specific problem you're trying to solve. Here are some common strategies:

1. Remove Missing Data

- **Drop Rows:**

  - Remove rows with missing values if the number of missing values is small relative to the dataset size.
  - Use pandas.DataFrame.dropna() in Python.
  - Example:

```python
df.dropna(inplace=True)
```

- **Drop Columns:**

  - Remove columns with a high percentage of missing values if they are not critical to the analysis.
  - Example:

```python
df.drop(columns=['column_name'], inplace=True)
```

When to Use:

- When the missing data is minimal and removing it does not significantly reduce the dataset size.
- When the missing data is not informative (e.g., missing completely at random).

2. Impute Missing Data
Imputation involves filling in missing values with estimated or calculated values. Common imputation methods include:
a. Mean/Median/Mode Imputation

- Replace missing values with the mean (for continuous data), median (for skewed data), or mode (for categorical data).
- Example (using pandas):

```python
df['column_name'].fillna(df['column_name'].mean(), inplace=True)
```
When to Use:

- When the data is numerical and missing values are small in number.

b. Forward Fill or Backward Fill

- Use the previous or next value in the dataset to fill missing values.
- Example:

```python
df['column_name'].fillna(method='ffill', inplace=True) # Forward fill
df['column_name'].fillna(method='bfill', inplace=True) # Backward fill
```
When to Use:

- For time-series data where the order of observations matters.

c. Interpolation

- Estimate missing values based on other values in the dataset (e.g., linear interpolation).
- Example:

python
df['column_name'].interpolate(method='linear', inplace=True)
When to Use:

- For time-series or sequential data with a clear trend.

d. K-Nearest Neighbors (KNN) Imputation

- Use the values of the nearest neighbors to estimate missing values.
- Example (using sklearn):

from sklearn.impute import KNNImputer
imputer = KNNImputer(n_neighbors=5)
df_imputed = imputer.fit_transform(df)
When to Use:

- When the dataset has a structure where nearby points are likely to have similar values.

e. Predictive Model Imputation

- Use a machine learning model (e.g., regression, decision trees) to predict missing values based on other features.
- Example:

  - Train a model on rows with no missing values and use it to predict missing values in other rows.

When to Use:

- When the missing data has a complex relationship with other features.

3. Use Algorithms That Handle Missing Data
Some algorithms, such as **XGBoost** and **LightGBM**, can handle missing data natively by learning the best imputation strategy during training.
When to Use:

- When you want to avoid manual imputation and let the algorithm handle missing values.

4. Flag Missing Data

- Create a new binary feature to indicate whether a value was missing in the original feature.
- Example:

```
df['column_name_missing'] = df['column_name'].isna().astype(int)
df['column_name'].fillna(df['column_name'].mean(), inplace=True)
```
When to Use:

- When the fact that data is missing might be informative (e.g., missing data is not random).

5. Advanced Techniques
a. Multiple Imputation

- Generate multiple imputed datasets, analyze each one, and combine the results.
- Example (using fancyimpute or statsmodels):

```
from fancyimpute import IterativeImputer
imputer = IterativeImputer()
df_imputed = imputer.fit_transform(df)
```
When to Use:

- When missing data is significant and you want to account for uncertainty in imputation.

b. Deep Learning-Based Imputation

- Use neural networks (e.g., autoencoders) to learn complex patterns and impute missing values.
- Example:

- ◦ Train an autoencoder on the dataset and use it to predict missing values.

When to Use:

- For large, complex datasets with non-linear relationships.

Choosing the Right Strategy

- **Understand the Cause of Missing Data:**

  - ◦ Is the data missing completely at random (MCAR), missing at random (MAR), or missing not at random (MNAR)?

- **Evaluate the Impact:**

  - ◦ How much data is missing, and how critical is the feature?

- **Consider the Algorithm:**

  - ◦ Does the algorithm you're using handle missing data natively?

- **Test and Validate:**

  - ◦ Compare the performance of different strategies using cross-validation.

Example Workflow in Python

```python
import pandas as pd
from sklearn.impute import SimpleImputer
# Load dataset
df = pd.read_csv('data.csv')
# Check for missing values
print(df.isnull().sum())
# Impute missing values with mean
imputer = SimpleImputer(strategy='mean')
df['column_name'] = imputer.fit_transform(df[['column_name']])
# Alternatively, use KNN imputation
```

```
from sklearn.impute import KNNImputer
imputer = KNNImputer(n_neighbors=5)
df_imputed             =             pd.DataFrame(imputer.fit_transform(df),
columns=df.columns)
```

Summary

- **Remove missing data** if it's minimal or not informative.
- **Impute missing data** using mean/median/mode, interpolation, KNN, or predictive models.
- **Use algorithms** that handle missing data natively.
- **Flag missing data** if its absence is informative.
- **Advanced techniques** like multiple imputation or deep learning can be used for complex datasets.

The choice of strategy depends on the nature of the data, the amount of missing values, and the specific requirements of the problem. Always validate the chosen approach to ensure it improves model performance.

Bagging and Boosting

Bagging and **Boosting** are two popular ensemble learning techniques used to improve the performance of machine learning models. Both methods combine multiple base models (e.g., decision trees) to create a stronger, more robust model, but they differ in their approach and underlying principles. Here's a detailed comparison:

Bagging (Bootstrap Aggregating)
How Bagging Works

1. **Bootstrap Sampling:**

   - Multiple subsets of the training data are created by randomly sampling with replacement (bootstrapping).
   - Each subset is used to train a separate base model (e.g., a decision tree).

2. **Parallel Training:**

   - All base models are trained independently and in parallel.

3. **Aggregation:**

   - For **classification**: The final prediction is made by majority voting (most frequent class) across all base models.
   - For **regression**: The final prediction is the average of predictions from all base models.

Key Characteristics

- **Reduces Variance**: Bagging reduces overfitting by averaging out the predictions, which helps stabilize the model.
- **Independent Models**: Base models are trained independently, making bagging suitable for parallel processing.
- **Examples**: Random Forest is a popular bagging algorithm.

Boosting
How Boosting Works

1. **Sequential Training**:

   - Base models are trained sequentially, where each model tries to correct the errors of the previous model.
   - Misclassified or poorly predicted instances are given more weight in subsequent iterations.

2. **Weighted Voting**:

   - For **classification**: The final prediction is a weighted majority vote, where better-performing models have higher weights.
   - For **regression**: The final prediction is a weighted average of predictions from all base models.

Key Characteristics

- **Reduces Bias**: Boosting focuses on reducing bias by iteratively improving the model's performance on difficult instances.
- **Dependent Models**: Each base model depends on the performance of the previous model, making boosting inherently sequential.
- **Examples**: AdaBoost, Gradient Boosting (GBM), XGBoost, LightGBM, and CatBoost.

Aspect	Bagging	Boosting
Training Approach	Parallel training of independent models.	Sequential training of dependent models.
Focus	Reduces variance and overfitting.	Reduces bias and improves accuracy.
Weighting of Data	All training instances are equally weighted.	Misclassified instances are given higher weight.
Model Aggregation	Averaging or majority voting.	Weighted voting or weighted averaging.
Performance	Works well with high-variance models (e.g., deep trees).	Works well with high-bias models (e.g., shallow trees).
Examples	Random Forest.	AdaBoost, Gradient Boosting, XGBoost.
Robustness to Noise	More robust to noise and outliers.	Less robust to noise and outliers.
Speed	Faster due to parallel training.	Slower due to sequential training.

Key Differences Between Bagging and Boosting

When to Use Bagging vs. Boosting
Use Bagging When:

- The base model is prone to overfitting (e.g., deep decision trees).
- You want to reduce variance and improve generalization.
- Parallel processing is preferred for faster training.

Use Boosting When:

- The base model is prone to underfitting (e.g., shallow decision trees).
- You want to reduce bias and improve accuracy.
- You have sufficient computational resources for sequential training.

Example of Bagging: Random Forest

```python
Copy
from sklearn.ensemble import RandomForestClassifier
from sklearn.datasets import load_iris
from sklearn.model_selection import train_test_split
from sklearn.metrics import accuracy_score
```

```python
# Load dataset
data = load_iris()
X, y = data.data, data.target
# Split data
X_train, X_test, y_train, y_test = train_test_split(X, y, test_size=0.3, random_state=42)
# Train Random Forest (Bagging)
model = RandomForestClassifier(n_estimators=100, random_state=42)
model.fit(X_train, y_train)
# Evaluate
y_pred = model.predict(X_test)
print("Accuracy:", accuracy_score(y_test, y_pred))
```

Example of Boosting: AdaBoost

python

Copy

```python
from sklearn.ensemble import AdaBoostClassifier
from sklearn.tree import DecisionTreeClassifier
from sklearn.datasets import load_iris
from sklearn.model_selection import train_test_split
from sklearn.metrics import accuracy_score
# Load dataset
data = load_iris()
X, y = data.data, data.target
# Split data
X_train, X_test, y_train, y_test = train_test_split(X, y, test_size=0.3, random_state=42)
# Train AdaBoost (Boosting)
base_model = DecisionTreeClassifier(max_depth=1)
model = AdaBoostClassifier(base_estimator=base_model, n_estimators=50, random_state=42)
model.fit(X_train, y_train)
# Evaluate
y_pred = model.predict(X_test)
print("Accuracy:", accuracy_score(y_test, y_pred))
```

Summary

- **Bagging** reduces variance by training independent models in parallel and aggregating their predictions.

- **Boosting** reduces bias by training models sequentially, with each model focusing on the errors of the previous one.
- Bagging is more robust to noise and faster to train, while boosting often achieves higher accuracy but is more sensitive to noise and slower to train.

Both techniques are powerful tools for improving model performance, and the choice between them depends on the specific problem and dataset.

## CHAPTER TWENTY

ROC (Receiver Operating Characteristic)

The **ROC (Receiver Operating Characteristic)** curve is a graphical representation of the performance of a binary classification model. It plots the **True Positive Rate (TPR)** against the **False Positive Rate (FPR)** at various classification thresholds. The ROC curve helps visualize the trade-off between sensitivity (recall) and specificity for a model.

Key Terms

1. **True Positive Rate (TPR) / Recall / Sensitivity:**

   ◦ Measures the proportion of actual positives correctly identified by the model.

2. **False Positive Rate (FPR):**

   ◦ Measures the proportion of actual negatives incorrectly identified as positives by the model.

3. **Threshold:**

   ◦ The cutoff probability used to classify an instance as positive or negative. For example, if the threshold is 0.5, probabilities ≥ 0.5 are classified as positive.

How the ROC Curve is Constructed

1. Vary the classification threshold from 0 to 1.

2. For each threshold, calculate TPR and FPR.
3. Plot TPR (y-axis) against FPR (x-axis).

Interpreting the ROC Curve

- **Diagonal Line (Random Guess):**

  - A diagonal line from (0,0) to (1,1) represents a model with no discriminative power (equivalent to random guessing).

- **Curve Above the Diagonal:**

  - The closer the ROC curve is to the top-left corner, the better the model's performance.
  - A perfect model has a TPR of 1 and an FPR of 0, resulting in a curve that passes through (0,1).

What is the AUC Score?

The **AUC (Area Under the Curve)** score is a single metric derived from the ROC curve. It represents the probability that a randomly chosen positive instance is ranked higher than a randomly chosen negative instance by the model. The AUC score ranges from 0 to 1:

- **AUC = 1**: Perfect classifier (all positives are ranked higher than negatives).
- **AUC = 0.5**: No discriminative power (equivalent to random guessing).
- **AUC > 0.5**: Better than random guessing.
- **AUC < 0.5**: Worse than random guessing (indicates the model is making systematic errors).

Interpreting the AUC Score

- **AUC = 0.9 - 1.0**: Excellent model.
- **AUC = 0.8 - 0.9**: Good model.
- **AUC = 0.7 - 0.8**: Fair model.
- **AUC = 0.6 - 0.7**: Poor model.
- **AUC = 0.5 - 0.6**: Fail model (no better than random guessing).

Advantages of ROC Curve and AUC Score

1. **Threshold Independence:**

   ○ The ROC curve and AUC score evaluate the model's performance across all possible thresholds, making them useful for comparing models without selecting a specific threshold.

2. **Imbalanced Data:**

   ○ The ROC curve and AUC score are robust to class imbalance, as they focus on the ranking of predictions rather than absolute values.

3. **Visual Interpretation:**

   ○ The ROC curve provides a visual representation of the trade-off between TPR and FPR, helping to select an optimal threshold based on the problem's requirements.

Example of ROC Curve and AUC in Python

```python
python
Copy
from sklearn.datasets import make_classification
from sklearn.model_selection import train_test_split
from sklearn.linear_model import LogisticRegression
from sklearn.metrics import roc_curve, roc_auc_score, auc
import matplotlib.pyplot as plt
# Generate synthetic dataset
X, y = make_classification(n_samples=1000, n_classes=2, random_state=42)
# Split data
X_train, X_test, y_train, y_test = train_test_split(X, y, test_size=0.3, random_state=42)
# Train a model
model = LogisticRegression()
model.fit(X_train, y_train)
# Predict probabilities
y_pred_proba = model.predict_proba(X_test)[:, 1]
```

```
# Calculate ROC curve
fpr, tpr, thresholds = roc_curve(y_test, y_pred_proba)
# Calculate AUC score
auc_score = roc_auc_score(y_test, y_pred_proba)
# Plot ROC curve
plt.figure()
plt.plot(fpr, tpr, color='blue', label=f'ROC Curve (AUC = {auc_score:.2f})')
plt.plot([0, 1], [0, 1], color='red', linestyle='--', label='Random Guess')
plt.xlabel('False Positive Rate (FPR)')
plt.ylabel('True Positive Rate (TPR)')
plt.title('ROC Curve')
plt.legend()
plt.show()
```

Summary

- The **ROC curve** plots TPR against FPR at various classification thresholds, providing a visual representation of a model's performance.
- The **AUC score** quantifies the area under the ROC curve and represents the model's ability to distinguish between positive and negative classes.
- A higher AUC score indicates better model performance, with 1 being perfect and 0.5 being no better than random guessing.
- The ROC curve and AUC score are widely used for evaluating and comparing binary classification models, especially in imbalanced datasets.

## CHAPTER TWENTY-ONE

L1 Regularization and L2 Regularization

L1 regularization and **L2 regularization** are two common techniques used to prevent overfitting in machine learning models by adding a penalty term to the cost function. While both methods aim to reduce the complexity of the model, they differ in how they penalize the model's parameters (weights). Here's a detailed comparison:

1. Definition

- **L1 Regularization (Lasso Regression):**

  - Adds the sum of the absolute values of the weights to the cost function.
  - Formula:

  $$\text{Cost} = \text{Original Cost} + \lambda \sum_{i=1}^{n} |w_i|$$

  where:

    - w_i = model weights,
    - λ = regularization parameter (controls the strength of regularization).

- **L2 Regularization (Ridge Regression):**

  - Adds the sum of the squared values of the weights to the cost function.
  - Formula:

Cost=Original Cost+λ∑i=1nwi2Cost=Original Cost+λi=1∑nwi2

2. Effect on Weights

- **L1 Regularization:**

  - Encourages sparsity by driving some weights to exactly zero.
  - Effectively performs feature selection by eliminating less important features.
  - Useful when you have many features and want to identify the most important ones.

- **L2 Regularization:**

  - Shrinks all weights proportionally but does not force them to zero.
  - Ensures that no single feature dominates the model.
  - Useful when all features are potentially relevant.

3. Geometric Interpretation

- **L1 Regularization:**

  - The penalty term forms a diamond-shaped constraint region (L1 norm).
  - The optimal solution often lies at the corners of the diamond, where some weights are zero.

- **L2 Regularization:**

  - The penalty term forms a circular constraint region (L2 norm).
  - The optimal solution lies somewhere on the boundary of the circle, where weights are small but non-zero.

4. Computational Complexity

- **L1 Regularization:**

  - More computationally expensive to solve because the absolute value function is not differentiable at zero.

- Requires specialized optimization algorithms (e.g., coordinate descent).

- **L2 Regularization:**

  - Easier to solve because the squared term is differentiable everywhere.
  - Can be optimized using standard gradient descent.

5. Robustness to Outliers

- **L1 Regularization:**

  - More robust to outliers because the absolute value term is less sensitive to large errors.

- **L2 Regularization:**

  - Less robust to outliers because the squared term amplifies the effect of large errors.

6. Use Cases

- **L1 Regularization:**

  - Feature selection: When you have a high-dimensional dataset with many irrelevant features.
  - Sparse models: When you want a model with fewer non-zero weights.

- **L2 Regularization:**

  - General-purpose regularization: When you want to prevent overfitting without eliminating features.
  - Correlated features: When features are highly correlated, L2 tends to distribute weight among them.

7. Mathematical Properties

- **L1 Regularization:**

- ○ Produces sparse solutions (many weights are exactly zero).
- ○ Non-differentiable at zero, which complicates optimization.

- **L2 Regularization:**

  - ○ Produces dense solutions (all weights are small but non-zero).
  - ○ Differentiable everywhere, making optimization easier.

8. Elastic Net: Combining L1 and L2

- **Elastic Net** is a hybrid approach that combines both L1 and L2 regularization.

When to Use L1 vs. L2

- Use **L1 regularization** when:

  - ○ You have a high-dimensional dataset with many irrelevant features.
  - ○ You want a sparse model with fewer non-zero weights.
  - ○ Feature selection is important.

- Use **L2 regularization** when:

  - ○ You want to prevent overfitting without eliminating features.
  - ○ All features are potentially relevant.
  - ○ You have correlated features and want to distribute weight among them.

- Use **Elastic Net** when:

  - ○ You want a balance between L1 and L2 regularization.
  - ○ You have many correlated features and want both sparsity and stability.

## CHAPTER TWENTY-TWO

Cross-validation

Cross-validation is a statistical technique used in machine learning to evaluate the performance of a model on an independent dataset. It involves partitioning the dataset into multiple subsets, training the model on some subsets, and validating it on the remaining subsets. This process is repeated multiple times to ensure that the model's performance is consistent and reliable.

The most common form of cross-validation is **k-fold cross-validation**, where the dataset is divided into **k** equal-sized folds. The model is trained on **k-1** folds and validated on the remaining fold. This process is repeated **k** times, with each fold used exactly once as the validation set. The final performance metric is typically the average of the metrics obtained from each fold.

Why is Cross-Validation Important?

Cross-validation is important for several reasons:

1. Reduces Overfitting

- Cross-validation helps ensure that the model generalizes well to unseen data by testing it on multiple subsets of the dataset.
- It prevents the model from memorizing the training data, which can lead to overfitting.

2. Provides a Robust Performance Estimate

- By averaging the performance across multiple folds, cross-validation provides a more reliable estimate of the model's performance compared to a single train-test split.
- It accounts for variability in the dataset, making the evaluation more stable.

3. Maximizes Data Utilization

- In traditional train-test splits, a portion of the data is reserved for testing, which reduces the amount of data available for training.
- Cross-validation uses the entire dataset for both training and validation, ensuring that no data is wasted.

4. Helps in Hyperparameter Tuning

- Cross-validation is often used in conjunction with techniques like grid search or random search to find the optimal hyperparameters for a model.
- It ensures that the selected hyperparameters generalize well to unseen data.

5. Detects Model Instability

- If a model performs well on some folds but poorly on others, it may indicate instability or sensitivity to specific subsets of the data.
- Cross-validation helps identify such issues, allowing for further investigation and improvement.

Types of Cross-Validation

1. **k-Fold Cross-Validation:**

   - The dataset is divided into **k** equal-sized folds.
   - The model is trained on **k-1** folds and validated on the remaining fold.
   - This process is repeated **k** times, with each fold used exactly once as the validation set.
   - Example: 5-fold cross-validation divides the data into 5 folds and repeats the process 5 times.

2. **Stratified k-Fold Cross-Validation:**

   - Used for classification problems with imbalanced classes.
   - Ensures that each fold has the same proportion of classes as the original dataset.

3. **Leave-One-Out Cross-Validation (LOOCV):**

    - A special case of k-fold cross-validation where **k = n** (number of samples).
    - Each sample is used once as the validation set, and the model is trained on the remaining **n-1** samples.
    - Computationally expensive but useful for small datasets.

4. **Time Series Cross-Validation:**

    - Used for time-series data where the order of observations matters.
    - Ensures that the model is validated on future data, simulating real-world scenarios.

Steps to Perform k-Fold Cross-Validation

1. **Split the Dataset:**

    - Divide the dataset into **k** equal-sized folds.

2. **Train and Validate:**

    - For each fold:

        - Use the fold as the validation set.
        - Train the model on the remaining **k-1** folds.
        - Evaluate the model on the validation set.

3. **Calculate Performance Metrics:**

    - Record the performance metric (e.g., accuracy, MSE) for each fold.

4. **Average the Metrics:**

    - Compute the average performance metric across all folds.

Example of k-Fold Cross-Validation

Suppose you have a dataset with 100 samples and you choose **k = 5**:

1. Split the data into 5 folds (20 samples each).
2. Train the model on folds 1-4 and validate on fold 5.
3. Repeat the process, training on folds 1, 2, 3, 5 and validating on fold 4.
4. Continue until each fold has been used as the validation set.
5. Average the performance metrics from all 5 folds to get the final evaluation.

Advantages of Cross-Validation

1. **Better Generalization:** Ensures the model performs well on unseen data.
2. **Reduced Bias:** Provides a more unbiased estimate of model performance compared to a single train-test split.
3. **Optimal Use of Data:** Utilizes the entire dataset for both training and validation.
4. **Hyperparameter Tuning:** Helps in selecting the best hyperparameters for the model.

Disadvantages of Cross-Validation

1. **Computationally Expensive:** Requires training the model multiple times, which can be time-consuming for large datasets or complex models.
2. **Not Suitable for All Data:** Time-series data or data with dependencies may require specialized cross-validation techniques.

When to Use Cross-Validation

- When you have a small dataset and want to maximize data utilization.
- When you need a robust estimate of model performance.
- When tuning hyperparameters to ensure they generalize well.
- When evaluating the stability and consistency of a model.

## CHAPTER TWENTY-THREE

Knowing Tensorflow

TensorFlow is one of the most popular open-source libraries for machine learning and deep learning, developed by Google. It is widely used for building and deploying machine learning models, especially neural networks. Below is a comprehensive guide to knowing TensorFlow, including its key features, components, and how to get started.

1. What is TensorFlow?

- Definition: TensorFlow is an end-to-end open-source platform for machine learning and deep learning.
- Purpose: It provides tools to build, train, and deploy machine learning models efficiently.
- Key Features:

  - Supports both CPU and GPU computation.
  - Scalable across multiple devices (e.g., mobile, edge devices, cloud).
  - Offers high-level APIs (e.g., Keras) for ease of use.
  - Provides flexibility for research and production.

2. Key Components of TensorFlow
a) Tensors

- Definition: Tensors are multi-dimensional arrays used to represent data in TensorFlow.
- Examples:

  - Scalar: 0-dimensional tensor (e.g., 5).
  - Vector: 1-dimensional tensor (e.g., [1, 2, 3]).
  - Matrix: 2-dimensional tensor (e.g., [[1, 2], [3, 4]]).

b) Graphs and Sessions

- Graph: A computational graph defines the operations (nodes) and tensors (edges) in a model.
- Session: A session runs the graph to execute operations and evaluate tensors.

c) Keras API

- Definition: A high-level API for building and training neural networks.
- Advantages:

    ◦ User-friendly and easy to learn.
    ◦ Integrates seamlessly with TensorFlow.

d) Eager Execution

- Definition: A mode that allows operations to be executed immediately (like Python code).
- Advantages:

    ◦ Easier debugging and development.
    ◦ More intuitive for beginners.

e) TensorFlow Extended (TFX)

- Definition: A production-ready platform for deploying machine learning pipelines.
- Components:

    ◦ Data validation.
    ◦ Model training and evaluation.
    ◦ Model serving.

f) TensorFlow Lite

- Definition: A lightweight version of TensorFlow for mobile and embedded devices.

- Use Cases:

  - Mobile apps.
  - IoT devices.

g) TensorFlow.js

- Definition: A JavaScript library for training and deploying models in the browser or Node.js.
- Use Cases:

  - Web-based machine learning applications.

3. Getting Started with TensorFlow
a) Installation

- Using pip:

```bash
Copy
pip install tensorflow
```

- For GPU support:

```bash
Copy
pip install tensorflow-gpu
```
b) Importing TensorFlow

- In Python:

```python
Copy
import tensorflow as tf
```
4. Building a Simple Neural Network with TensorFlow
Example: MNIST Handwritten Digit Classification
python
Copy

```python
import tensorflow as tf
from tensorflow.keras import layers, models
# Load the MNIST dataset
mnist = tf.keras.datasets.mnist
(x_train, y_train), (x_test, y_test) = mnist.load_data()
# Normalize the data
x_train, x_test = x_train / 255.0, x_test / 255.0
# Build the model
model = models.Sequential([
layers.Flatten(input_shape=(28, 28)), # Input layer
layers.Dense(128, activation='relu'), # Hidden layer
layers.Dropout(0.2), # Dropout for regularization
layers.Dense(10, activation='softmax') # Output layer
])
# Compile the model
model.compile(optimizer='adam',
loss='sparse_categorical_crossentropy',
metrics=['accuracy'])
# Train the model
model.fit(x_train, y_train, epochs=5)
# Evaluate the model
model.evaluate(x_test, y_test)
```

5. Key TensorFlow Concepts

a) Layers

- Definition: Building blocks of neural networks (e.g., Dense, Conv2D, LSTM).
- Example:

```python
Copy
layer = tf.keras.layers.Dense(units=64, activation='relu')
```

b) Optimizers

- Definition: Algorithms to minimize the loss function (e.g., Adam, SGD).
- Example:

```python
python
```

```
Copy
optimizer = tf.keras.optimizers.Adam(learning_rate=0.001)
```
c) Loss Functions

- Definition: Measures the difference between predicted and actual values.
- Examples:

    - tf.keras.losses.MeanSquaredError() (for regression).
    - tf.keras.losses.SparseCategoricalCrossentropy() (for classification).

d) Metrics

- Definition: Used to evaluate model performance (e.g., accuracy, precision).
- Example:

```python
Copy
metrics = ['accuracy']
```
e) Callbacks

- Definition: Functions executed during training (e.g., early stopping, model checkpointing).
- Example:

```python
Copy
callbacks = [tf.keras.callbacks.EarlyStopping(patience=2)]
```
6. Advanced TensorFlow Features
a) Custom Models

- Definition: Create custom models by subclassing tf.keras.Model.
- Example:

```python
Copy
class MyModel(tf.keras.Model):
def __init__(self):
```

```python
super(MyModel, self).__init__()
self.dense1 = layers.Dense(64, activation='relu')
self.dense2 = layers.Dense(10, activation='softmax')
def call(self, inputs):
x = self.dense1(inputs)
return self.dense2(x)
```

b) Custom Training Loops

- Definition: Write custom training loops for more control over the training process.
- Example:

```python
python
Copy
for epoch in range(epochs):
for x_batch, y_batch in dataset:
with tf.GradientTape() as tape:
predictions = model(x_batch)
loss = loss_fn(y_batch, predictions)
gradients = tape.gradient(loss, model.trainable_variables)
optimizer.apply_gradients(zip(gradients, model.trainable_variables))
```

c) TensorBoard

- Definition: A visualization tool for monitoring training and debugging models.
- Usage:

```python
python
Copy
tensorboard_callback = tf.keras.callbacks.TensorBoard(log_dir='./logs')
model.fit(x_train, y_train, epochs=5, callbacks=[tensorboard_callback])
```

## CHAPTER TWENTY-FOUR

Confusion Matrix

A **confusion matrix** is a table used to evaluate the performance of a classification model by comparing the model's predictions against the actual (true) labels. It provides a detailed breakdown of correct and incorrect predictions, making it a powerful tool for understanding the model's performance, especially in binary and multi-class classification problems.

Structure of a Confusion Matrix

For a **binary classification** problem, the confusion matrix is a 2x2 table with the following components:

Predicted Positive

Predicted Negative

Actual Positive

True Positive (TP)

False Negative (FN)

Actual Negative

False Positive (FP)

True Negative (TN)

- **True Positive (TP):** The model correctly predicted the positive class.
- **False Positive (FP):** The model incorrectly predicted the positive class (actual was negative).
- **False Negative (FN):** The model incorrectly predicted the negative class (actual was positive).
- **True Negative (TN):** The model correctly predicted the negative class.

For **multi-class classification**, the confusion matrix is an $n \times n$ table, where n is the number of classes. Each row represents the actual class, and each column represents the predicted class.

How to Interpret a Confusion Matrix

The confusion matrix provides insights into the model's performance by highlighting:

1. **Correct Predictions:**

   - **True Positives (TP)** and **True Negatives (TN)** indicate where the model is performing well.

2. **Incorrect Predictions:**

   - **False Positives (FP)** and **False Negatives (FN)** indicate where the model is making errors.

Key Metrics Derived from a Confusion Matrix

From the confusion matrix, several important performance metrics can be calculated:

1. **Accuracy:**

   - Measures the overall correctness of the model.
   -

1. **Precision:**

   - Measures the proportion of correctly predicted positive instances out of all predicted positive instances.
   -

3. **Recall (Sensitivity or True Positive Rate):**

   - Measures the proportion of correctly predicted positive instances out of all actual positive instances.

4. **F1-Score:**

   - The harmonic mean of precision and recall, providing a balance between the two.
   -

5. **Specificity (True Negative Rate):**

   - Measures the proportion of correctly predicted negative instances out
   - of all actual negative instances.

6. **False Positive Rate (FPR):**

   - Measures the proportion of actual negatives incorrectly predicted as positives.

Aspect	Precision	Recall
Definition	Proportion of correct positive predictions.	Proportion of actual positives correctly predicted.
Focus	Minimizing **false positives (FP)**.	Minimizing **false negatives (FN)**.
Use Case	When FP is costly (e.g., spam detection).	When FN is costly (e.g., disease detection).
Trade-off	High precision often leads to lower recall	High recall often leads to lower precision.

Key Differences

When to Use Precision vs. Recall

- **Precision** is more important when the goal is to minimize false positives (e.g., spam detection, recommendation systems).
- **Recall** is more important when the goal is to minimize false negatives (e.g., disease detection, fraud detection).

In practice, the choice between precision and recall depends on the specific problem and the relative costs of false positives and false negatives. Often, a balance between the two is sought using metrics like the **F1-Score**, which is the harmonic mean of precision and recall.

## CHAPTER TWENTY-FIVE

Feature Engineering

1. What is Feature Engineering?

- Definition: The process of creating new features or modifying existing ones to improve model performance.
- Purpose: To make the data more suitable for machine learning algorithms by highlighting important patterns and relationships.
- Importance:

  ◦ Improves model accuracy.
  ◦ Reduces overfitting.
  ◦ Enhances interpretability.

2. Steps in Feature Engineering
a) Data Understanding

- Analyze the dataset to understand its structure, distribution, and relationships.
- Identify the types of data (e.g., numerical, categorical, text).

b) Data Cleaning

- Handle missing values, outliers, and inconsistencies.
- Remove irrelevant or redundant features.

c) Feature Creation

- Create new features from existing data.
- Example: Derive "age" from "date of birth."

d) Feature Transformation

- Transform features to make them more suitable for modeling.
- Example: Normalize numerical features.

e) Feature Selection

- Select the most relevant features to reduce dimensionality and improve model performance.

3. Feature Engineering Techniques
a) Handling Missing Data

- Imputation: Fill missing values with mean, median, mode, or a constant.

```python
Copy
from sklearn.impute import SimpleImputer
imputer = SimpleImputer(strategy='mean')
X_imputed = imputer.fit_transform(X)
```

- Deletion: Remove rows or columns with missing values.

```python
Copy
df.dropna(inplace=True)
b) Encoding Categorical Data
```

- One-Hot Encoding: Convert categories into binary vectors.

```python
Copy
import pandas as pd
data = pd.DataFrame({'color': ['red', 'blue', 'green']})
encoded_data = pd.get_dummies(data)
```

- Label Encoding: Assign a unique integer to each category.

```
python
Copy
from sklearn.preprocessing import LabelEncoder
encoder = LabelEncoder()
data['color_encoded'] = encoder.fit_transform(data['color'])
c) Scaling Numerical Data
```

- Normalization: Scale values to a range (e.g., [0, 1]).

```
python
Copy
from sklearn.preprocessing import MinMaxScaler
scaler = MinMaxScaler()
X_scaled = scaler.fit_transform(X)
```

- Standardization: Scale values to have a mean of 0 and a standard deviation of 1.

```
python
Copy
from sklearn.preprocessing import StandardScaler
scaler = StandardScaler()
X_scaled = scaler.fit_transform(X)
d) Feature Extraction
```

- Principal Component Analysis (PCA): Reduce dimensionality while preserving variance.

```
python
Copy
from sklearn.decomposition import PCA
pca = PCA(n_components=2)
X_pca = pca.fit_transform(X)
```

- Text Feature Extraction:

  - Bag of Words (BoW): Represent text as a vector of word frequencies.

```
python
Copy
from sklearn.feature_extraction.text import CountVectorizer
vectorizer = CountVectorizer()
X = vectorizer.fit_transform(['I love machine learning', 'Machine learning is fun'])
```

- TF-IDF: Represent text based on word importance.

```
python
Copy
from sklearn.feature_extraction.text import TfidfVectorizer
vectorizer = TfidfVectorizer()
X = vectorizer.fit_transform(['I love machine learning', 'Machine learning is fun'])
```

e) Feature Creation

- Polynomial Features: Create interaction terms and polynomial features.

```
python
Copy
from sklearn.preprocessing import PolynomialFeatures
poly = PolynomialFeatures(degree=2)
X_poly = poly.fit_transform(X)
```

- Binning: Convert continuous features into discrete bins.

```
python
Copy
import pandas as pd
df['age_bin'] = pd.cut(df['age'], bins=[0, 18, 35, 60, 100], labels=['child', 'young', 'adult', 'senior'])
```

- Date/Time Features:

  - Extract day, month, year, or day of the week from a date.

```
python
```

Copy
df['year'] = df['date'].dt.year
df['month'] = df['date'].dt.month
f) Feature Interaction

- Create new features by combining existing ones.

python
Copy
df['total_income'] = df['salary'] + df['bonus']
4. Feature Selection Techniques
a) Filter Methods

- Select features based on statistical measures.
- Examples:

  - Correlation coefficient.
  - Chi-square test.
  - Mutual information.

b) Wrapper Methods

- Use a subset of features to train a model and evaluate performance.
- Examples:

  - Recursive Feature Elimination (RFE).
  - Forward/backward selection.

c) Embedded Methods

- Select features during the model training process.
- Examples:

  - Lasso regularization (L1).
  - Decision tree feature importance.

5. Tools for Feature Engineering
a) Python Libraries

- Pandas: For data manipulation and cleaning.
- NumPy: For numerical operations.
- Scikit-learn: For preprocessing and feature selection.
- Featuretools: For automated feature engineering.

b) Visualization Tools

- Matplotlib/Seaborn: For data visualization.
- Tableau/Power BI: For interactive data exploration.

6. Best Practices for Feature Engineering

1. Understand the Data: Analyze the dataset to identify patterns and relationships.
2. Iterate and Experiment: Try different feature engineering techniques and evaluate their impact.
3. Avoid Data Leakage: Ensure that feature engineering is done separately on training and test datasets.
4. Collaborate with Domain Experts: Leverage domain knowledge to create meaningful features.
5. Document Your Process: Keep track of the features created and the transformations applied.

By mastering feature engineering, you can significantly improve the performance of your machine learning models and uncover hidden insights in your data. Happy feature engineering!

## CHAPTER TWENTY-SIX

Classification and Regression

Classification and **regression** are two fundamental types of supervised learning tasks in machine learning. They differ primarily in the nature of the output they predict and the type of problems they are used to solve. Here's a detailed comparison:

1. Definition

- **Classification:**

    - Predicts discrete class labels (categories).
    - The output is a finite set of values (e.g., binary: 0 or 1; multi-class: cat, dog, bird).
    - Example: Predicting whether an email is spam or not spam.

- **Regression:**

    - Predicts continuous numerical values.
    - The output is a real number (e.g., price, temperature, age).
    - Example: Predicting the price of a house based on its features.

2. Type of Output

- **Classification:**

    - Output is categorical (discrete).
    - Examples: Binary classification (yes/no, true/false), multi-class classification (red/blue/green).

- **Regression:**

- ◦ Output is continuous.
- ◦ Examples: Predicting stock prices, temperature, or sales revenue.

3. Algorithms

- **Classification:**

  - ◦ Algorithms are designed to predict discrete labels.
  - ◦ Common algorithms:

    - Logistic Regression (despite its name, it's used for classification).
    - Decision Trees.
    - Random Forest.
    - Support Vector Machines (SVM).
    - k-Nearest Neighbors (k-NN).
    - Neural Networks.

- **Regression:**

  - ◦ Algorithms are designed to predict continuous values.
  - ◦ Common algorithms:

    - Linear Regression.
    - Polynomial Regression.
    - Ridge Regression.
    - Lasso Regression.
    - Decision Trees (can also be used for regression).
    - Random Forest (for regression tasks).
    - Neural Networks.

4. Evaluation Metrics

- **Classification:**

  - ◦ Metrics focus on the accuracy of predicted classes.
  - ◦ Common metrics:

    - Accuracy.

- Precision, Recall, and F1-Score.
- Confusion Matrix.
- ROC-AUC (Receiver Operating Characteristic - Area Under Curve).

- **Regression:**

  - Metrics focus on the difference between predicted and actual values.
  - Common metrics:

    - Mean Absolute Error (MAE).
    - Mean Squared Error (MSE).
    - Root Mean Squared Error (RMSE).
    - R-squared (R^2).

5. Use Cases

- **Classification:**

  - Used when the goal is to assign input data to specific categories.
  - Examples:

    - Spam detection (spam or not spam).
    - Image recognition (identifying objects in images).
    - Medical diagnosis (disease or no disease).
    - Sentiment analysis (positive, negative, neutral).

- **Regression:**

  - Used when the goal is to predict a continuous quantity.
  - Examples:

    - Predicting house prices.
    - Forecasting stock prices.
    - Estimating temperature or rainfall.
    - Predicting sales revenue.

6. Mathematical Formulation

- **Classification:**

  - The output is a probability distribution over classes.
  - Example: Logistic regression uses the sigmoid function to output probabilities between 0 and 1.

- **Regression:**

  - The output is a direct numerical value.
  - Example: Linear regression models the relationship between input features and the output using a linear equation.

7. Visualization

- **Classification:**

  - Visualized using decision boundaries (e.g., a line separating two classes in 2D space).
  - Example: A scatter plot with points colored by their predicted class.

- **Regression:**

  - Visualized using a best-fit line or curve.
  - Example: A scatter plot with a line showing the relationship between input and output variables.

8. Example Problem

- **Classification:**

  - Problem: Predict whether a customer will churn (leave) or not.
  - Input: Customer demographics, usage patterns.
  - Output: "Churn" or "No Churn."

- **Regression:**

  - Problem: Predict the monthly spending of a customer.
  - Input: Customer demographics, past spending behavior.

- Output: A numerical value representing the predicted spending.

Aspect	Classification	Regression
Output Type	Discrete (categories)	Continuous (numerical values)
Goal	Assign input to a category	Predict a numerical value
Algorithms	Logistic Regression, SVM, Decision Trees	Linear Regression, Ridge, Lasso
Evaluation Metrics	Accuracy, Precision, Recall, F1-Score, AUC	MAE, MSE, RMSE, R-squared
Use Cases	Spam detection, image recognition	House price prediction, stock forecasting
Visualization	Decision boundaries	Best-fit line or curve

Summary Table

k-Nearest Neighbors (KNN)

The **k-Nearest Neighbors (KNN)** algorithm is a simple, instance-based supervised learning algorithm used for both **classification** and **regression** tasks. It operates on the principle that similar data points (neighbors) tend to have similar outcomes. Here's how it works:

Step-by-Step Working of KNN

1. **Input Data:**

   - The algorithm requires a labeled dataset with features (independent variables) and corresponding labels (dependent variable).

2. **Choose the Value of kk:**

   - kk is a user-defined parameter representing the number of nearest neighbors to consider when making a prediction.

3. **Calculate Distance:**

   - For a new data point (query point), KNN calculates the distance between this point and all other points in the dataset.
   - Common distance metrics include:

     - **Euclidean Distance**
     - **Manhattan Distance**
     - **Minkowski Distance:** A generalized form of Euclidean and Manhattan distances.

4. **Find the kk Nearest Neighbors:**

- Identify the k data points in the training set that are closest to the query point based on the calculated distances.

5. **Make a Prediction:**

   - For **classification**: The predicted class is the majority class among the k nearest neighbors.
   - For **regression**: The predicted value is the average (or weighted average) of the target values of the k nearest neighbors.

6. **Output the Result:**

   - Return the predicted class (classification) or value (regression) for the query point.

Example of KNN in Action

Suppose you have a dataset of flowers with two features: petal length and petal width. The goal is to classify a new flower as either "Setosa" or "Versicolor."

1. Choose $k=3$.
2. Calculate the Euclidean distance between the new flower and all flowers in the dataset.
3. Identify the 3 nearest neighbors.
4. If 2 out of the 3 neighbors are "Setosa," predict the new flower as "Setosa."

Limitations of KNN

While KNN is simple and effective in many cases, it has several limitations:

1. **Computationally Expensive:**

   - KNN requires calculating the distance between the query point and every point in the dataset, which can be slow for large datasets.
   - No explicit training phase, but prediction time increases with dataset size.

2. **Sensitive to the Choice of kk:**

   - A small kk can lead to overfitting (high variance), as the model becomes too sensitive to noise.
   - A large kk can lead to underfitting (high bias), as the model may oversimplify the decision boundary.

3. **Sensitive to Feature Scaling:**

   - Features with larger scales can dominate the distance calculation, leading to biased results. Normalization or standardization is often required.

4. **Curse of Dimensionality:**

   - KNN performs poorly in high-dimensional spaces because the distance metric becomes less meaningful as the number of dimensions increases.

5. **Imbalanced Data:**

   - In classification tasks, if one class dominates the dataset, the majority class may disproportionately influence the prediction.

6. **Memory Intensive:**

   - KNN stores the entire dataset in memory, which can be problematic for very large datasets.

7. **No Model Interpretation:**

   - KNN is a non-parametric algorithm, meaning it does not provide insights into the relationship between features and the target variable.

When to Use KNN

Despite its limitations, KNN can be a good choice in the following scenarios:

- Small to medium-sized datasets.
- Low-dimensional data.
- When interpretability is not a priority.
- When the decision boundary is highly irregular.

Improvements to KNN

To address some of its limitations, the following techniques can be applied:

- Use **approximate nearest neighbor (ANN)** algorithms for faster search in large datasets.
- Apply **feature scaling** to normalize the data.
- Use **dimensionality reduction** techniques (e.g., PCA) to handle high-dimensional data.
- Choose an optimal kk using cross-validation.

In summary, KNN is a simple and intuitive algorithm but has limitations related to computational efficiency, scalability, and sensitivity to hyperparameters and data characteristics.

## CHAPTER TWENTY-EIGHT

Support Vector Machine (SVM)

Support Vector Machine (SVM) is a powerful supervised learning algorithm used for both **classification** and **regression** tasks. It is particularly effective in high-dimensional spaces and is widely used for binary classification. Here's how it works:

Key Concepts

1. **Hyperplane:**

    ◦ In a binary classification problem, SVM finds the optimal hyperplane that separates the two classes.
    ◦ A hyperplane is a decision boundary in n-dimensional space, where n is the number of features.

2. **Support Vectors:**

    ◦ Support vectors are the data points closest to the hyperplane and influence its position and orientation.
    ◦ These points are critical in defining the margin and the decision boundary.

3. **Margin:**

    ◦ The margin is the distance between the hyperplane and the nearest data points (support vectors) from either class.
    ◦ SVM aims to maximize this margin to improve generalization.

Step-by-Step Working of SVM

1. **Input Data:**

   - SVM takes labeled training data as input, where each data point belongs to one of two classes.

2. **Find the Optimal Hyperplane:**

   - SVM identifies the hyperplane that maximizes the margin between the two classes.
   - The hyperplane is defined by the equation:

   $w \cdot x + b = 0$ $w \cdot x + b = 0$
   where:

     - w w is the weight vector.
     - x x is the feature vector.
     - b b is the bias term.

2. **Maximize the Margin:**

   - The margin is maximized by minimizing the norm of the weight vector w w, subject to the constraint that all data points are correctly classified (or within a soft margin for non-separable data).

3. **Classification:**

   - For a new data point, SVM predicts the class based on which side of the hyperplane the point lies:

   $\text{Class} = \text{sign}(w \cdot x + b)$ $\text{Class} = \text{sign}(w \cdot x + b)$
   Role of the Kernel in SVM
   The **kernel** is a key component of SVM that enables it to handle non-linearly separable data. It transforms the input data into a higher-dimensional space where a linear hyperplane can separate the classes.
   Why Kernels are Needed

- In many real-world problems, data is not linearly separable in its original feature space.
- Kernels allow SVM to find a non-linear decision boundary by mapping the data to a higher-dimensional space where linear separation is possible.

Common Kernel Functions

1. **Linear Kernel:**

   - Used for linearly separable data.
   - Formula:

   $$K(x_i,x_j)=x_i \cdot x_j \quad K(x_i,x_j)=x_i \cdot x_j$$

2. **Polynomial Kernel:**

   - Captures polynomial relationships between features.
   - Formula:

   $$K(x_i,x_j)=(\gamma x_i \cdot x_j+r)^d \quad K(x_i,x_j)=(\gamma x_i \cdot x_j+r)^d$$
   where:

     - γ: Kernel coefficient.
     - r: Constant term.
     - d: Degree of the polynomial.

3. **Radial Basis Function (RBF) Kernel:**

   - Most commonly used kernel for non-linear data.
   - Formula:

   $$K(x_i,x_j)=\exp\left(-\gamma \| x_i-x_j \|^2\right) \quad K(x_i,x_j)=\exp(-\gamma \| x_i-x_j \|^2)$$
   where:

     - γ: Controls the influence of individual data points.

4. **Sigmoid Kernel:**

   - Mimics the behavior of a neural network.
   - Formula:

$$K(xi,xj)=\tanh(\gamma xi \cdot xj+r) K(xi,xj)=\tanh(\gamma xi \cdot xj+r)$$

Kernel Trick

- The kernel trick allows SVM to operate in a high-dimensional space without explicitly computing the coordinates of the data in that space.
- Instead, it computes the inner product between pairs of data points in the transformed space, which is computationally efficient.

Advantages of SVM

1. **Effective in High-Dimensional Spaces:**

   - SVM performs well even when the number of features exceeds the number of samples.

2. **Robust to Overfitting:**

   - By maximizing the margin, SVM reduces the risk of overfitting, especially in high-dimensional spaces.

3. **Versatile:**

   - The use of kernels makes SVM suitable for both linear and non-linear classification tasks.

4. **Global Optimal Solution:**

   - SVM finds the globally optimal solution, unlike some other algorithms that may get stuck in local optima.

Limitations of SVM

1. **Computationally Expensive:**

- ◦ Training time can be high for large datasets.

2. **Sensitive to Noise:**

   - ◦ Outliers can significantly affect the position of the hyperplane.

3. **Choice of Kernel and Parameters:**

   - ◦ Selecting the right kernel and tuning parameters (e.g., CC, $\gamma\gamma$) can be challenging.

Example of SVM in Python (scikit-learn)

```python
from sklearn.datasets import make_classification
from sklearn.model_selection import train_test_split
from sklearn.svm import SVC
from sklearn.metrics import accuracy_score
# Generate synthetic dataset
X, y = make_classification(n_samples=1000, n_features=20, random_state=42)
# Split data
X_train, X_test, y_train, y_test = train_test_split(X, y, test_size=0.3, random_state=42)
# Train SVM with RBF kernel
model = SVC(kernel='rbf', gamma='scale', random_state=42)
model.fit(X_train, y_train)
# Evaluate
y_pred = model.predict(X_test)
print("Accuracy:", accuracy_score(y_test, y_pred))
```

Summary

- SVM finds the optimal hyperplane to separate data points of different classes while maximizing the margin.
- Kernels enable SVM to handle non-linearly separable data by transforming it into a higher-dimensional space.
- Common kernels include linear, polynomial, RBF, and sigmoid.
- SVM is effective in high-dimensional spaces and robust to overfitting but can be computationally expensive and sensitive to parameter choices.

## CHAPTER TWENTY-NINE

Decision Tree

A **Decision Tree** is a supervised machine learning algorithm used for both **classification** and **regression** tasks. It works by splitting the dataset into subsets based on feature values, creating a tree-like structure of decisions. Here's how it works:

Step-by-Step Working of Decision Trees

1. **Start at the Root Node:**

   ○ The algorithm begins with the entire dataset at the root node.

2. **Select the Best Feature to Split:**

   ○ The algorithm selects the feature that best separates the data into distinct classes or reduces impurity (for classification) or variance (for regression).
   ○ Common criteria for selecting the best feature:

     ▪ **Classification:** Gini Impurity, Information Gain, or Entropy.
     ▪ **Regression:** Reduction in Variance.

3. **Split the Dataset:**

   ○ The dataset is split into subsets based on the selected feature's values.
   ○ Each subset corresponds to a branch of the tree.

4. **Repeat the Process:**

- The algorithm recursively applies the same process to each subset, creating child nodes.
- This continues until a stopping condition is met (e.g., maximum depth, minimum samples per leaf, or no further improvement in purity).

5. **Leaf Nodes:**

- The final nodes (leaf nodes) represent the predicted class (classification) or value (regression).

Example of a Decision Tree

Suppose you want to predict whether a person will play tennis based on features like Outlook, Temperature, Humidity, and Wind. A decision tree might look like this:

1. **Root Node:** Outlook

- If Outlook = Sunny:

  - Check Humidity.

    - If Humidity ≤ 70: Play Tennis.
    - Else: Don't Play Tennis.

- If Outlook = Overcast: Play Tennis.
- If Outlook = Rainy:

  - Check Wind.

    - If Wind = Weak: Play Tennis.
    - Else: Don't Play Tennis.

Handling Overfitting in Decision Trees

Decision trees are prone to **overfitting**, especially when they grow too deep and capture noise in the training data. Overfitting results in a model that performs well on the training data but poorly on unseen data. Here are some strategies to handle overfitting:

1. Pruning

- **Pruning** involves removing branches of the tree that do not provide significant predictive power.
- **Pre-Pruning (Early Stopping)**:

  - Stop the tree-growing process before it reaches maximum depth.
  - Use parameters like:

    - max_depth: Limit the maximum depth of the tree.
    - min_samples_split: Minimum number of samples required to split a node.
    - min_samples_leaf: Minimum number of samples required at a leaf node.

- **Post-Pruning**:

  - Grow the tree fully and then remove unnecessary branches.
  - Use techniques like **Cost Complexity Pruning** (e.g., ccp_alpha in scikit-learn).

2. Limit Tree Depth

- Restrict the maximum depth of the tree using the max_depth parameter.
- A smaller tree is less likely to overfit.

3. Set Minimum Samples for Splits and Leaves

- Use parameters like min_samples_split and min_samples_leaf to control the number of samples required for splitting a node or forming a leaf.
- This prevents the tree from creating nodes with very few samples, which are likely to capture noise.

4. Use Ensemble Methods

- Combine multiple decision trees to reduce overfitting:

- ○ **Random Forests**: Build multiple trees on random subsets of the data and features, then average their predictions.
- ○ **Gradient Boosting**: Sequentially build trees, where each tree corrects the errors of the previous one.

5. Cross-Validation

- Use cross-validation to tune hyperparameters (e.g., max_depth, min_samples_split) and ensure the model generalizes well to unseen data.

6. Feature Selection

- Remove irrelevant or redundant features to simplify the tree and reduce overfitting.

7. Regularization

- Use regularization techniques like **Cost Complexity Pruning** (CCP), which adds a penalty for tree complexity.
- The ccp_alpha parameter in scikit-learn controls the trade-off between tree complexity and accuracy.

## CHAPTER THIRTY

Random Forest

Random Forest is an ensemble learning method that combines multiple decision trees to improve predictive performance and reduce overfitting. It belongs to the **bagging** family of algorithms and is widely used for both **classification** and **regression** tasks. Here's how it works:

Step-by-Step Working of Random Forest

1. **Bootstrap Sampling**:

   ○ Random subsets of the training data are created by sampling with replacement (bootstrapping).
   ○ Each subset is used to train a separate decision tree.

2. **Feature Randomness**:

   ○ At each split in a decision tree, only a random subset of features is considered (instead of all features).
   ○ This introduces diversity among the trees and reduces correlation between them.

3. **Train Individual Trees**:

   ○ Each decision tree is trained independently on its bootstrap sample and feature subset.
   ○ The trees are grown to their maximum depth (no pruning).

4. **Aggregate Predictions**:

- ○ For **classification**: The final prediction is made by majority voting (most frequent class) across all trees.
- ○ For **regression**: The final prediction is the average of predictions from all trees.

Why Random Forest is Better Than a Single Decision Tree
Random Forest improves upon a single decision tree in several ways:
1. Reduces Overfitting

- A single decision tree tends to overfit the training data, especially when it grows too deep.
- Random Forest reduces overfitting by averaging the predictions of multiple trees, which smooths out the noise and captures the underlying patterns better.

2. Improves Generalization

- By combining the predictions of multiple trees, Random Forest produces a more robust and stable model that generalizes better to unseen data.

3. Handles High Variance

- A single decision tree can have high variance, meaning small changes in the training data can lead to significantly different trees.
- Random Forest reduces variance by aggregating the results of multiple trees trained on different subsets of the data.

4. Feature Importance

- Random Forest provides a measure of feature importance by evaluating how much each feature contributes to the model's performance across all trees.
- This helps in understanding the dataset and selecting relevant features.

5. Handles Missing Data and Outliers

- Random Forest is more robust to missing data and outliers compared to a single decision tree because it averages the predictions of multiple trees.

6. No Need for Pruning

- Individual trees in a Random Forest are grown to their maximum depth without pruning, which simplifies the training process.
- The ensemble approach naturally controls overfitting, eliminating the need for pruning.

7. Parallelizable

- Since each tree is trained independently, Random Forest can be easily parallelized, making it computationally efficient for large datasets.

Example of Random Forest in Python (scikit-learn)
```python
from sklearn.ensemble import RandomForestClassifier
from sklearn.datasets import load_iris
from sklearn.model_selection import train_test_split
from sklearn.metrics import accuracy_score
# Load dataset
data = load_iris()
X, y = data.data, data.target
# Split data
X_train, X_test, y_train, y_test = train_test_split(X, y, test_size=0.3, random_state=42)
# Train Random Forest
model = RandomForestClassifier(n_estimators=100, random_state=42)
model.fit(X_train, y_train)
# Evaluate
y_pred = model.predict(X_test)
print("Accuracy:", accuracy_score(y_test, y_pred))
```
Key Parameters in Random Forest

1. **n_estimators**: Number of trees in the forest (more trees generally improve performance but increase computation time).
2. **max_features**: Number of features to consider at each split (e.g., sqrt or log2 of total features).
3. **max_depth**: Maximum depth of each tree (controls tree complexity).
4. **min_samples_split**: Minimum number of samples required to split a node.

5. **min_samples_leaf**: Minimum number of samples required at a leaf node.
6. **bootstrap**: Whether to use bootstrap sampling (default is True).

Summary

- Random Forest is an ensemble method that combines multiple decision trees to improve predictive performance.
- It reduces overfitting, improves generalization, and handles high variance better than a single decision tree.
- Key advantages include robustness to noise, handling missing data, feature importance, and parallelizability.
- Random Forest is widely used in practice due to its simplicity, accuracy, and versatility.

## CHAPTER THIRTY-ONE

Handling Time-series Data

Handling time-series data in machine learning requires special considerations because of its temporal nature. Time-series data is a sequence of data points collected or recorded at specific time intervals, and it often exhibits trends, seasonality, and dependencies over time. Here's a step-by-step guide to handling time-series data effectively:

1. Understand the Problem

- **Forecasting**: Predicting future values (e.g., stock prices, weather).
- **Anomaly Detection**: Identifying unusual patterns (e.g., fraud detection, equipment failure).
- **Classification**: Categorizing time-series data (e.g., activity recognition, ECG classification).

2. Preprocess the Data

- **Handle Missing Values:**

  - Use interpolation, forward fill, or backward fill to impute missing values.
  - Example:

```python
df['value'].interpolate(method='linear', inplace=True)
```

- **Resampling:**

  - Convert data to a consistent frequency (e.g., daily, hourly).
  - Example:

df.resample('D').mean() # Resample to daily frequency

- **Smooth the Data:**

    ◦ Apply rolling averages or exponential smoothing to reduce noise.
    ◦ Example:

df['value'].rolling(window=7).mean() # 7-day rolling average

- **Remove Trends and Seasonality:**

    ◦ Use differencing or decomposition to make the data stationary.
    ◦ Example:

df['value_diff'] = df['value'].diff() # First-order differencing

3. Feature Engineering

- **Create Time-Based Features:**

    ◦ Extract features like hour, day, month, year, day of the week, etc.
    ◦ Example:

df['hour'] = df.index.hour
df['day_of_week'] = df.index.dayofweek

- **Lag Features:**

    ◦ Include past values as features to capture temporal dependencies.
    ◦ Example:

df['lag_1'] = df['value'].shift(1) # Lag of 1 time step

- **Rolling Statistics:**

    ◦ Compute rolling means, variances, or other statistics.
    ◦ Example:

df['rolling_mean'] = df['value'].rolling(window=7).mean()

- **Domain-Specific Features:**

  - Incorporate features specific to the problem (e.g., holidays, events).

4. Split the Data

- **Time-Based Split:**

  - Split the data into training and testing sets based on time (e.g., train on the first 80% and test on the last 20%).
  - Example:

```
train_size = int(len(df) * 0.8)
train, test = df[:train_size], df[train_size:]
```

- **Avoid Random Splits:**

  - Random splits can lead to data leakage, as future data may influence the model.

5. Choose the Right Model

- **Traditional Models:**

  - **ARIMA (AutoRegressive Integrated Moving Average):** For stationary time-series data.
  - **Exponential Smoothing (Holt-Winters):** For data with trends and seasonality.

- **Machine Learning Models:**

  - **Linear Regression:** With lag features and time-based features.
  - **Random Forest, Gradient Boosting:** With engineered features.
  - **Support Vector Machines (SVM):** For smaller datasets.

- **Deep Learning Models:**

- **Recurrent Neural Networks (RNNs):** For capturing long-term dependencies.
- **Long Short-Term Memory (LSTM):** A type of RNN for long sequences.
- **Convolutional Neural Networks (CNNs):** For feature extraction in time-series data.

6. Evaluate the Model

- **Metrics for Forecasting:**

  - Mean Absolute Error (MAE), Mean Squared Error (MSE), Root Mean Squared Error (RMSE).

- **Metrics for Classification:**

  - Accuracy, Precision, Recall, F1-Score.

- **Backtesting:**

  - Evaluate the model on multiple time periods to ensure robustness.

7. Handle Seasonality and Trends

- **Decomposition:**

  - Use techniques like STL (Seasonal and Trend decomposition using Loess) to separate trend, seasonality, and residuals.

- **Differencing:**

  - Subtract the previous value from the current value to remove trends.
  - Example:

```
df['value_diff'] = df['value'].diff()
```

8. Use Cross-Validation for Time-Series

- **TimeSeriesSplit:**

- ○ Use time-series cross-validation to evaluate the model on multiple time periods.
- ○ Example:

```
from sklearn.model_selection import TimeSeriesSplit
tscv = TimeSeriesSplit(n_splits=5)
for train_index, test_index in tscv.split(df):
    train, test = df.iloc[train_index], df.iloc[test_index]
```

9. Deploy and Monitor

- **Deploy the Model:**

  - ○ Use the trained model to make predictions on new data.

- **Monitor Performance:**

  - ○ Continuously monitor the model's performance and retrain as needed.

Example Workflow in Python

```
import pandas as pd
from sklearn.model_selection import TimeSeriesSplit
from sklearn.ensemble import RandomForestRegressor
from sklearn.metrics import mean_squared_error
# Load time-series data
df = pd.read_csv('time_series_data.csv', parse_dates=['date'],
index_col='date')
# Feature engineering
df['lag_1'] = df['value'].shift(1)
df['rolling_mean'] = df['value'].rolling(window=7).mean()
df.dropna(inplace=True)
# Split data
train_size = int(len(df) * 0.8)
train, test = df[:train_size], df[train_size:]
# Train model
X_train, y_train = train.drop(columns=['value']), train['value']
X_test, y_test = test.drop(columns=['value']), test['value']
model = RandomForestRegressor()
```

```
model.fit(X_train, y_train)
# Evaluate
y_pred = model.predict(X_test)
print("RMSE:", mean_squared_error(y_test, y_pred, squared=False))
```

Summary

- **Preprocess the data**: Handle missing values, resample, and smooth.
- **Engineer features**: Create time-based, lag, and rolling features.
- **Split the data**: Use time-based splits to avoid data leakage.
- **Choose the right model**: Use traditional, machine learning, or deep learning models.
- **Evaluate the model**: Use appropriate metrics and cross-validation.
- **Handle seasonality and trends**: Use decomposition or differencing.
- **Deploy and monitor**: Continuously monitor the model's performance.

By following these steps, you can effectively handle time-series data and build robust machine learning models.

## CHAPTER THIRTY-TWO

Advancement of AI

The advancement of Artificial Intelligence (AI) has been one of the most transformative technological developments of the 21st century. From its theoretical beginnings in the 1950s to its current state-of-the-art applications, AI has evolved significantly. Below is a detailed explanation of the key advancements in AI, organized into historical milestones, technological breakthroughs, and future trends.

1. Historical Milestones in AI Advancement

a) The Birth of AI (1950s - 1960s)

- 1950: Alan Turing proposes the Turing Test to evaluate a machine's ability to exhibit intelligent behavior.
- 1956: The term "Artificial Intelligence" is coined at the Dartmouth Conference, marking the official birth of AI as a field.
- 1957: Frank Rosenblatt develops the Perceptron, an early neural network model.
- 1960s: Early AI programs like the General Problem Solver (GPS) and ELIZA (a chatbot) demonstrate symbolic reasoning and natural language processing.

b) The AI Winter (1970s - 1980s)

- 1970s: Progress slows due to limited computational power and unrealistic expectations, leading to the first AI Winter (a period of reduced funding and interest).
- 1980s: Expert systems (rule-based AI) gain popularity in industries like medicine and finance, but their limitations lead to another AI Winter in the late 1980s.

c) The Rise of Machine Learning (1990s - 2000s)

- 1997: IBM's Deep Blue defeats world chess champion Garry Kasparov, showcasing AI's potential in strategic decision-making.
- 2006: Geoffrey Hinton introduces deep learning techniques, reviving interest in neural networks.
- 2009: The rise of big data and advancements in computational power (e.g., GPUs) enable the training of large-scale AI models.

d) The Deep Learning Revolution (2010s)

- 2012: AlexNet, a deep convolutional neural network, wins the ImageNet competition, revolutionizing computer vision.
- 2014: Generative Adversarial Networks (GANs) are introduced, enabling AI to generate realistic images, videos, and audio.
- 2016: Google's AlphaGo defeats world champion Lee Sedol in the game of Go, demonstrating AI's ability to master complex tasks.
- 2018: OpenAI's GPT (Generative Pre-trained Transformer) models advance natural language processing (NLP).

e) The Era of Generative AI (2020s)

- 2020: OpenAI releases GPT-3, a language model with 175 billion parameters, capable of generating human-like text.
- 2022: AI art generators like DALL·E 2 and Stable Diffusion gain popularity, enabling the creation of high-quality images from text prompts.
- 2023: ChatGPT and other conversational AI systems become mainstream, transforming industries like customer service, education, and healthcare.

2. Key Technological Advancements in AI
a) Deep Learning

- Breakthrough: The development of deep neural networks with multiple layers.
- Impact: Enabled significant improvements in computer vision, speech recognition, and natural language processing.

- Examples:

    ◦ Convolutional Neural Networks (CNNs) for image recognition.
    ◦ Recurrent Neural Networks (RNNs) and Transformers for NLP.

b) Reinforcement Learning

- Breakthrough: Algorithms that learn by interacting with an environment and receiving rewards or penalties.
- Impact: Used to develop AI systems that can master complex games and control tasks.
- Examples:

    ◦ AlphaGo and AlphaZero (game-playing AI).
    ◦ Robotics and autonomous systems.

c) Generative AI

- Breakthrough: Models that can generate new data (e.g., text, images, audio) based on patterns learned from existing data.
- Impact: Revolutionized creative industries and content generation.
- Examples:

    ◦ GPT models for text generation.
    ◦ DALL·E and Stable Diffusion for image generation.

d) Transfer Learning

- Breakthrough: Techniques that allow pre-trained models to be fine-tuned for new tasks with minimal data.
- Impact: Reduced the need for large datasets and computational resources.
- Examples:

    ◦ Fine-tuning GPT for specific NLP tasks.
    ◦ Using pre-trained vision models for medical image analysis.

e) Edge AI

- Breakthrough: Running AI models on edge devices (e.g., smartphones, IoT devices) instead of centralized servers.
- Impact: Enabled real-time AI applications with low latency and improved privacy.
- Examples:

  - Facial recognition on smartphones.
  - Autonomous drones and vehicles.

3. Applications of Advanced AI
a) Healthcare

- Diagnostics: AI systems can analyze medical images (e.g., X-rays, MRIs) to detect diseases like cancer.
- Drug Discovery: AI accelerates the identification of potential drug candidates.
- Personalized Medicine: AI tailors treatments based on individual patient data.

b) Autonomous Systems

- Self-Driving Cars: Companies like Tesla, Waymo, and Uber use AI for navigation and decision-making.
- Drones: AI-powered drones are used for delivery, surveillance, and agriculture.

c) Natural Language Processing (NLP)

- Chatbots: AI-powered chatbots like ChatGPT provide customer support and assistance.
- Language Translation: Tools like Google Translate use AI to translate text and speech in real-time.
- Sentiment Analysis: AI analyzes social media and customer feedback to gauge public opinion.

d) Finance

- Fraud Detection: AI identifies suspicious transactions and prevents fraud.
- Algorithmic Trading: AI analyzes market data to make trading decisions.
- Credit Scoring: AI assesses creditworthiness based on historical data.

e) Creative Industries

- Art and Music: AI generates paintings, music, and other creative works.
- Content Creation: AI writes articles, scripts, and marketing copy.

4. Future Trends in AI Advancement
a) Artificial General Intelligence (AGI)

- Definition: AI systems that can perform any intellectual task that a human can do.
- Challenges: Requires breakthroughs in reasoning, learning, and adaptability.
- Potential Impact: Could revolutionize industries and solve complex global problems.

b) Explainable AI (XAI)

- Definition: AI systems that provide transparent and interpretable decisions.
- Importance: Critical for building trust and ensuring ethical AI use.
- Applications: Healthcare, finance, and legal systems.

c) AI Ethics and Regulation

- Focus: Ensuring AI systems are fair, unbiased, and accountable.
- Initiatives: Governments and organizations are developing frameworks for responsible AI use.

d) Quantum AI

- Definition: Combining AI with quantum computing to solve complex problems.

- Potential: Could revolutionize fields like cryptography, optimization, and drug discovery.

e) AI for Sustainability

- Applications: Using AI to address climate change, optimize energy use, and manage natural resources.
- Examples: AI-powered smart grids, precision agriculture, and wildlife conservation.

5. Challenges in AI Advancement
a) Ethical Concerns

- Bias in AI models.
- Privacy issues with data collection.
- Potential misuse of AI (e.g., deepfakes, autonomous weapons).

b) Technical Limitations

- High computational costs.
- Difficulty in achieving AGI.
- Lack of interpretability in complex models.

c) Societal Impact

- Job displacement due to automation.
- Widening the digital divide.
- Ensuring equitable access to AI technologies.

Predicting the state of Artificial Intelligence (AI) in 2050 involves a mix of extrapolating current trends, understanding technological limitations, and considering societal and ethical implications. While it's impossible to predict the future with certainty, we can explore potential scenarios based on advancements in AI research, computing power, and global trends. Here's a comprehensive look at what AI might look like in 2050:

1. Technological Advancements in AI by 2050
a) Artificial General Intelligence (AGI)

- Definition: AI systems that can perform any intellectual task that a human can do.
- Potential: By 2050, AGI could become a reality, enabling machines to reason, learn, and adapt across diverse domains.
- Impact:

  - Revolutionize industries by automating complex decision-making tasks.
  - Solve global challenges like climate change, disease, and poverty.

b) Superintelligent AI

- Definition: AI that surpasses human intelligence in all aspects.
- Potential: If achieved, superintelligent AI could outperform humans in creativity, problem-solving, and scientific discovery.
- Impact:

  - Accelerate technological and scientific breakthroughs.
  - Raise ethical concerns about control and safety.

c) Brain-Computer Interfaces (BCIs)

- Definition: Direct communication between the human brain and AI systems.
- Potential: By 2050, BCIs could enable seamless interaction with AI, enhancing human cognition and capabilities.
- Impact:

  - Enable paralyzed individuals to control devices with their thoughts.
  - Augment human intelligence and memory.

d) Quantum AI

- Definition: Combining AI with quantum computing to solve complex problems.
- Potential: Quantum AI could revolutionize fields like cryptography, optimization, and drug discovery.
- Impact:

- ◦ Solve problems that are currently intractable for classical computers.
- ◦ Enable breakthroughs in materials science and energy.

2. Applications of AI in 2050
a) Healthcare

- Personalized Medicine: AI could tailor treatments to individual genetic profiles, lifestyles, and environments.
- Disease Prevention: AI-powered wearable devices could monitor health in real-time and predict diseases before symptoms appear.
- Robotic Surgeons: Autonomous robots could perform complex surgeries with precision and minimal human intervention.

b) Education

- Personalized Learning: AI could create customized learning plans for students based on their strengths, weaknesses, and interests.
- Virtual Tutors: AI-powered tutors could provide 24/7 assistance and adapt to each student's learning style.
- Lifelong Learning: AI could enable continuous skill development and career transitions in a rapidly changing job market.

c) Transportation

- Autonomous Vehicles: Self-driving cars, trucks, and drones could dominate transportation, reducing accidents and improving efficiency.
- Smart Cities: AI could optimize traffic flow, reduce emissions, and manage public transportation systems.

d) Environment and Sustainability

- Climate Modeling: AI could improve climate predictions and help design strategies to mitigate global warming.
- Resource Management: AI could optimize the use of water, energy, and agricultural resources.
- Wildlife Conservation: AI could monitor endangered species and combat poaching using drones and sensors.

e) Space Exploration

- Autonomous Spacecraft: AI could enable unmanned missions to explore distant planets and moons.
- Space Colonization: AI could assist in building and maintaining habitats on the Moon, Mars, and beyond.

3. Societal and Economic Impact of AI in 2050
a) Workforce Transformation

- Automation: AI could automate most repetitive and manual jobs, leading to significant shifts in the job market.
- New Jobs: New roles in AI development, ethics, and human-AI collaboration could emerge.
- Universal Basic Income (UBI): Governments might implement UBI to address job displacement and ensure economic stability.

b) Human-AI Collaboration

- Augmented Intelligence: AI could enhance human capabilities, enabling people to achieve more in less time.
- Creative Partnerships: AI could collaborate with humans in art, music, and scientific research, leading to new forms of creativity.

c) Ethical and Legal Frameworks

- AI Regulation: Governments and organizations could establish robust frameworks to ensure ethical AI use.
- Bias and Fairness: AI systems could be designed to minimize bias and ensure fairness across diverse populations.
- Privacy: Advanced encryption and data protection measures could safeguard personal information in an AI-driven world.

4. Challenges and Risks of AI in 2050
a) Ethical Concerns

- Autonomous Weapons: The development of AI-powered weapons could lead to new forms of warfare.

- Surveillance: AI could enable mass surveillance, raising concerns about privacy and civil liberties.
- Inequality: Unequal access to AI technologies could widen the gap between developed and developing nations.

b) Technical Challenges

- Control and Safety: Ensuring that superintelligent AI systems remain under human control.
- Robustness: Developing AI systems that are reliable and resilient to failures or adversarial attacks.
- Energy Consumption: Addressing the high energy demands of advanced AI systems.

c) Societal Impact

- Job Displacement: Automation could lead to widespread unemployment and social unrest.
- Human Identity: The integration of AI into daily life could challenge traditional notions of what it means to be human.
- Cultural Shifts: AI could influence cultural norms, values, and behaviors in unpredictable ways.

5. Scenarios for AI in 2050
a) Optimistic Scenario

- AI for Good: AI is used to solve global challenges, improve quality of life, and enhance human potential.
- Collaborative Future: Humans and AI work together harmoniously, with AI augmenting human capabilities.
- Equitable Access: AI technologies are distributed fairly, benefiting all of humanity.

b) Pessimistic Scenario

- Loss of Control: Superintelligent AI systems act in ways that are misaligned with human values.

- Economic Disruption: Widespread job displacement leads to social and economic instability.
- Ethical Failures: AI systems perpetuate bias, discrimination, and inequality.

c) Balanced Scenario

- Regulated AI: Governments and organizations establish ethical guidelines and regulations to ensure responsible AI use.
- Adaptive Workforce: Societies adapt to AI-driven changes by investing in education and reskilling programs.
- Human-Centric AI: AI systems are designed to prioritize human well-being and ethical considerations.

6. Key Questions for AI in 2050

- Will AGI be achieved, and how will it impact society?
- How can we ensure that AI systems are safe, ethical, and aligned with human values?
- What role will governments, businesses, and individuals play in shaping the future of AI?
- How can we address the challenges of job displacement and economic inequality in an AI-driven world?
- What new forms of creativity, collaboration, and innovation will emerge from human-AI partnerships?

## CHAPTER THIRTY-THREE

Staying Updated

Staying updated with the latest advancements in machine learning is crucial for keeping your skills relevant and leveraging cutting-edge techniques in your projects. Here are some effective strategies to stay informed:

1. Follow Research Papers and Journals

- **arXiv:**

  - A repository of preprint research papers in machine learning, AI, and related fields.
  - Website: arxiv.org

- **Google Scholar:**

  - A search engine for scholarly articles and research papers.
  - Website: scholar.google.com

- **Conference Proceedings:**

  - Follow proceedings from top conferences like NeurIPS, ICML, CVPR, ICLR, and ACL.

2. Subscribe to Newsletters and Blogs

- **Towards Data Science:**

  - A Medium publication with articles on machine learning and data science.
  - Website: towardsdatascience.com

- **KDnuggets:**

  - A leading site for AI, machine learning, and data science news.
  - Website: kdnuggets.com

- **The Batch by DeepLearning.AI:**

  - A weekly newsletter covering the latest in AI and machine learning.
  - Website: deeplearning.ai/the-batch

- **Distill:**

  - A platform for clear and insightful explanations of machine learning research.
  - Website: distill.pub

3. Attend Conferences and Meetups

- **Conferences:**

  - Attend major conferences like NeurIPS, ICML, CVPR, ICLR, and ACL.

- **Meetups:**

  - Join local or virtual meetups to network with professionals and learn about new trends.
  - Website: meetup.com

4. Take Online Courses and Tutorials

- **Coursera:**

  - Offers courses from top universities and organizations.
  - Website: coursera.org

- **edX:**

  - Provides courses from institutions like MIT, Harvard, and Berkeley.

- ◦ Website: <u>edx.org</u>

- **Fast.ai**:

  - ◦ Offers practical deep learning courses.
  - ◦ Website: <u>fast.ai</u>

- **Udacity**:

  - ◦ Provides nanodegree programs in AI and machine learning.
  - ◦ Website: <u>udacity.com</u>

5. Follow Influential Researchers and Practitioners

- **Twitter**:

  - ◦ Follow leading researchers and practitioners like Yann LeCun, Andrew Ng, Fei-Fei Li, and Ian Goodfellow.

- **LinkedIn**:

  - ◦ Connect with professionals and join AI/ML groups for discussions and updates.

6. Participate in Competitions

- **Kaggle**:

  - ◦ Participate in machine learning competitions to apply your skills and learn from others.
  - ◦ Website: <u>kaggle.com</u>

- **DrivenData**:

  - ◦ Competitions focused on social impact.
  - ◦ Website: <u>drivendata.org</u>

7. Read Books and Textbooks

- **Deep Learning by Ian Goodfellow, Yoshua Bengio, and Aaron Courville:**

  - A comprehensive textbook on deep learning.

- **Pattern Recognition and Machine Learning by Christopher M. Bishop:**

  - A foundational text on machine learning.

- **Hands-On Machine Learning with Scikit-Learn, Keras, and TensorFlow by Aurélien Géron:**

  - A practical guide to machine learning.

8. Join Online Communities and Forums

- **Reddit:**

  - Join subreddits like r/MachineLearning, r/datascience, and r/learnmachinelearning.
  - Website: reddit.com

- **Stack Overflow:**

  - Participate in discussions and ask questions.
  - Website: stackoverflow.com

- **GitHub:**

  - Explore and contribute to open-source machine learning projects.
  - Website: github.com

9. Experiment with Open-Source Tools and Frameworks

- **TensorFlow:**

  - Experiment with the latest features and models.
  - Website: tensorflow.org

- **PyTorch:**

  - Explore cutting-edge research implementations.
  - Website: pytorch.org

- **Hugging Face:**

  - Work with state-of-the-art NLP models.
  - Website: huggingface.co

10. Listen to Podcasts and Watch Videos

- **Podcasts:**

  - Listen to podcasts like "Data Skeptic," "The AI Podcast," and "TWiML & AI."

- **YouTube:**

  - Follow channels like Two Minute Papers, Yannic Kilcher, and DeepMind.

11. Engage in Continuous Learning

- **MOOCs:**

  - Enroll in massive open online courses (MOOCs) to learn new skills.

- **Workshops and Webinars:**

  - Attend workshops and webinars hosted by universities, companies, and organizations.

12. Contribute to Open Source

- **GitHub:**

- ◦ Contribute to open-source projects to gain hands-on experience and collaborate with others.

- **OpenAI:**

  - ◦ Explore and contribute to OpenAI's research and projects.
  - ◦ Website: <u>openai.com</u>

Summary

- **Research Papers**: Follow arXiv, Google Scholar, and conference proceedings.
- **Newsletters**: Subscribe to Towards Data Science, KDnuggets, and The Batch.
- **Conferences**: Attend NeurIPS, ICML, CVPR, ICLR, and ACL.
- **Courses**: Take courses on Coursera, edX, Fast.ai, and Udacity.
- **Influencers**: Follow researchers on Twitter and LinkedIn.
- **Competitions**: Participate in Kaggle and DrivenData competitions.
- **Books**: Read foundational and practical books on machine learning.
- **Communities**: Join Reddit, Stack Overflow, and GitHub communities.
- **Tools**: Experiment with TensorFlow, PyTorch, and Hugging Face.
- **Podcasts**: Listen to AI and machine learning podcasts.
- **Continuous Learning**: Engage in MOOCs, workshops, and webinars.
- **Open Source**: Contribute to open-source projects.

By leveraging these resources and strategies, you can stay updated with the latest advancements in machine learning and continuously improve your skills.

## CHAPTER THIRTY-FOUR

Projects for Learning Machine Learning

Learning machine learning (ML) is best done through hands-on projects that allow you to apply theoretical concepts to real-world problems. Below is a curated list of machine learning projects for beginners, intermediate learners, and advanced practitioners. These projects cover a wide range of topics, from basic algorithms to cutting-edge techniques.

Beginner-Level Projects

These projects are ideal for those new to machine learning and focus on foundational concepts and algorithms.

1. Titanic Survival Prediction

- Description: Predict whether a passenger survived the Titanic disaster using features like age, gender, and class.
- Skills Learned: Data preprocessing, classification, and evaluation metrics (accuracy, precision, recall).
- Dataset: Titanic Dataset on Kaggle.

2. Iris Flower Classification

- Description: Classify iris flowers into species based on sepal and petal measurements.
- Skills Learned: Supervised learning, classification, and visualization.
- Dataset: Iris Dataset.

3. House Price Prediction

- Description: Predict house prices using features like size, location, and number of rooms.
- Skills Learned: Regression, feature engineering, and model evaluation (RMSE, MAE).
- Dataset: Boston Housing Dataset.

4. Spam Email Detection

- Description: Build a model to classify emails as spam or not spam.
- Skills Learned: Text preprocessing, NLP, and classification.
- Dataset: Spam Email Dataset.

5. Handwritten Digit Recognition

- Description: Recognize handwritten digits (0-9) using the MNIST dataset.
- Skills Learned: Image processing, classification, and neural networks.
- Dataset: MNIST Dataset.

Intermediate-Level Projects
These projects are for learners who have a basic understanding of ML and want to explore more complex algorithms and techniques.
6. Customer Segmentation

- Description: Group customers into segments based on purchasing behavior using clustering algorithms.
- Skills Learned: Unsupervised learning, clustering (K-means, DBSCAN), and visualization.
- Dataset: Mall Customer Segmentation Dataset.

7. Sentiment Analysis

- Description: Analyze the sentiment of movie reviews (positive or negative).
- Skills Learned: NLP, text classification, and deep learning (RNNs, LSTMs).
- Dataset: IMDB Movie Reviews Dataset.

8. Credit Card Fraud Detection

- Description: Detect fraudulent credit card transactions using anomaly detection techniques.
- Skills Learned: Imbalanced datasets, anomaly detection, and evaluation metrics (precision, recall, F1-score).
- Dataset: Credit Card Fraud Detection Dataset.

9. Stock Price Prediction

- Description: Predict future stock prices using historical data.
- Skills Learned: Time series analysis, regression, and deep learning (LSTMs).
- Dataset: Yahoo Finance.

10. Image Classification with CNN

- Description: Build a convolutional neural network (CNN) to classify images (e.g., cats vs. dogs).
- Skills Learned: Image processing, CNNs, and transfer learning.
- Dataset: Cats vs. Dogs Dataset.

Advanced-Level Projects
These projects are for experienced learners who want to tackle complex problems and explore cutting-edge techniques.

11. Object Detection

- Description: Detect and localize objects in images using models like YOLO or Faster R-CNN.
- Skills Learned: Object detection, deep learning, and computer vision.
- Dataset: COCO Dataset.

12. Generative Adversarial Networks (GANs)

- Description: Generate realistic images using GANs (e.g., faces, artwork).
- Skills Learned: GANs, deep learning, and image generation.
- Dataset: CelebA Dataset.

13. Chatbot Development

- Description: Build a conversational chatbot using NLP and deep learning.
- Skills Learned: Sequence-to-sequence models, transformers, and NLP.
- Dataset: Cornell Movie Dialogues Corpus.

14. Recommender System

- Description: Build a movie or product recommendation system using collaborative filtering or matrix factorization.
- Skills Learned: Recommender systems, collaborative filtering, and matrix factorization.
- Dataset: MovieLens Dataset.

15. Self-Driving Car Simulation

- Description: Train a model to drive a car in a simulated environment using reinforcement learning.
- Skills Learned: Reinforcement learning, deep learning, and simulation.
- Tools: OpenAI Gym or CARLA Simulator.

Specialized Projects
These projects focus on niche areas of machine learning and advanced applications.
16. Medical Diagnosis

- Description: Predict diseases (e.g., diabetes, cancer) using patient data.
- Skills Learned: Classification, feature engineering, and healthcare applications.
- Dataset: Pima Indians Diabetes Dataset.

17. Music Generation

- Description: Generate music using deep learning models like LSTMs or transformers.
- Skills Learned: Sequence modeling, deep learning, and creativity.
- Dataset: MAESTRO Dataset.

18. Fake News Detection

- Description: Classify news articles as real or fake using NLP techniques.
- Skills Learned: Text classification, NLP, and deep learning.
- Dataset: Fake News Dataset.

19. Human Activity Recognition

- Description: Classify human activities (e.g., walking, running) using sensor data.
- Skills Learned: Time series analysis, classification, and feature engineering.
- Dataset: UCI HAR Dataset.

20. Language Translation

- Description: Build a language translation model using sequence-to-sequence models or transformers.
- Skills Learned: NLP, sequence modeling, and deep learning.
- Dataset: WMT Dataset.

Tools and Libraries for Machine Learning Projects

- Python Libraries:

  - Scikit-learn (for traditional ML algorithms).
  - TensorFlow and PyTorch (for deep learning).
  - Pandas and NumPy (for data manipulation).
  - Matplotlib and Seaborn (for visualization).

- Platforms:

  - Kaggle (for datasets and competitions).
  - Google Colab (for free GPU/TPU access).
  - Jupyter Notebook (for interactive coding).

Tips for Success

1. Start Small: Begin with beginner-level projects and gradually move to more complex ones.
2. Focus on Understanding: Don't just copy code; understand the underlying concepts.
3. Experiment: Try different algorithms, hyperparameters, and techniques.
4. Document Your Work: Keep a record of your experiments, results, and learnings.
5. Collaborate: Join online communities like Kaggle or GitHub to share and learn from others.

## CHAPTER THIRTY-FIVE

Machine Learning Interview Questions

Here are some common machine learning interview questions along with their answers:

1. What is Machine Learning?

- Answer: Machine Learning (ML) is a subset of artificial intelligence (AI) that involves training algorithms to learn patterns from data and make predictions or decisions without being explicitly programmed. It uses statistical techniques to enable machines to improve their performance on a task with experience.

2. What are the types of Machine Learning?

- Answer: There are three main types:

  1. Supervised Learning: The model is trained on labeled data (input-output pairs). Examples include regression and classification.
  2. Unsupervised Learning: The model is trained on unlabeled data to find patterns or groupings. Examples include clustering and dimensionality reduction.
  3. Reinforcement Learning: The model learns by interacting with an environment and receiving rewards or penalties for actions.

3. What is the difference between supervised and unsupervised learning?

- Answer:

- Supervised Learning: Uses labeled data to train the model. The goal is to predict the output for new inputs.
- Unsupervised Learning: Uses unlabeled data to find hidden patterns or intrinsic structures in the data.

4. What is overfitting, and how can you prevent it?

- Answer: Overfitting occurs when a model learns the training data too well, capturing noise and outliers, which harms its performance on unseen data.
- Prevention:

  - Use more training data.
  - Apply regularization techniques (e.g., L1/L2 regularization).
  - Simplify the model (e.g., reduce the number of features or use pruning in decision trees).
  - Use cross-validation.
  - Apply dropout in neural networks.

5. What is the bias-variance tradeoff?

- Answer:

  - Bias: Error due to overly simplistic assumptions in the learning algorithm. High bias can cause underfitting.
  - Variance: Error due to the model's sensitivity to small fluctuations in the training set. High variance can cause overfitting.
  - The tradeoff involves balancing bias and variance to minimize total error.

6. What is cross-validation, and why is it important?

- Answer: Cross-validation is a technique to evaluate a model's performance by splitting the data into multiple subsets, training on some, and validating on others. Common methods include k-fold cross-validation.
- Importance: It helps ensure the model generalizes well to unseen data and reduces the risk of overfitting.

7. Explain the difference between classification and regression.

- Answer:

  - Classification: Predicts discrete labels (e.g., spam or not spam).
  - Regression: Predicts continuous values (e.g., house prices).

8. What is a confusion matrix?

- Answer: A confusion matrix is a table used to evaluate the performance of a classification model. It shows:

  - True Positives (TP)
  - True Negatives (TN)
  - False Positives (FP)
  - False Negatives (FN)

- Metrics like accuracy, precision, recall, and F1-score can be derived from it.

9. What is the ROC curve, and what does AUC mean?

- Answer:

  - ROC Curve: A plot of the True Positive Rate (TPR) vs. False Positive Rate (FPR) at various thresholds.
  - AUC (Area Under Curve): Measures the model's ability to distinguish between classes. AUC ranges from 0 to 1, where 1 is perfect classification.

10. What is gradient descent?

- Answer: Gradient descent is an optimization algorithm used to minimize the loss function by iteratively adjusting the model's parameters in the direction of the steepest descent (negative gradient).

11. What is the difference between bagging and boosting?

- Answer:

    - Bagging (Bootstrap Aggregating): Trains multiple models independently on random subsets of data and averages their predictions (e.g., Random Forest).
    - Boosting: Trains models sequentially, where each model corrects the errors of the previous one (e.g., AdaBoost, Gradient Boosting).

12. What is a decision tree, and how does it work?

- Answer: A decision tree is a tree-like model where each internal node represents a decision based on a feature, each branch represents an outcome, and each leaf node represents a class label or value. It splits the data recursively based on feature values to maximize information gain or minimize impurity.

13. What is the difference between L1 and L2 regularization?

- Answer:

    - L1 Regularization (Lasso): Adds the absolute value of coefficients to the loss function. It can shrink some coefficients to zero, performing feature selection.
    - L2 Regularization (Ridge): Adds the squared value of coefficients to the loss function. It shrinks coefficients but does not set them to zero.

14. What is a neural network?

- Answer: A neural network is a computational model inspired by the human brain. It consists of layers of interconnected nodes (neurons) that process input data and learn to perform tasks like classification or regression.

15. What is the difference between deep learning and machine learning?

- Answer: Deep learning is a subset of machine learning that uses neural networks with many layers (deep architectures) to learn complex patterns in data. Machine learning includes a broader range of algorithms, including simpler models like linear regression.

16. What is a support vector machine (SVM)?

- Answer: SVM is a supervised learning algorithm used for classification and regression. It finds the optimal hyperplane that separates data points of different classes with the maximum margin.

17. What is the curse of dimensionality?

- Answer: As the number of features (dimensions) increases, the data becomes sparse, making it harder for models to learn patterns effectively. This can lead to overfitting and increased computational complexity.

18. What is the difference between precision and recall?

- Answer:

  - Precision: The ratio of true positives to the total predicted positives (TP / (TP + FP)).
  - Recall: The ratio of true positives to the total actual positives (TP / (TP + FN)).

19. What is k-means clustering?

- Answer: K-means is an unsupervised learning algorithm that partitions data into k clusters by minimizing the variance within each cluster. It iteratively assigns data points to the nearest centroid and updates the centroids.

20. What is the difference between generative and discriminative models?

- Answer:

  - Generative Models: Learn the joint probability distribution of inputs and outputs (e.g., Naive Bayes, GANs).

- Discriminative Models: Learn the conditional probability of outputs given inputs (e.g., Logistic Regression, SVM).

These questions cover a broad range of topics in machine learning. Be prepared to explain concepts in detail and provide examples or practical applications where relevant.

machine learning 100 interview questions with answers

Here's a comprehensive list of 100 machine learning interview questions along with their answers. These questions cover fundamental concepts, algorithms, and practical applications of machine learning.

Basic Concepts

1. What is Machine Learning?

   - Answer: Machine Learning is a subset of AI that enables systems to learn from data and improve their performance on a task without being explicitly programmed.

2. What are the types of Machine Learning?

   - Answer: Supervised, Unsupervised, Reinforcement Learning.

3. What is supervised learning?

   - Answer: Training a model on labeled data (input-output pairs) to predict outputs for new inputs.

4. What is unsupervised learning?

   - Answer: Training a model on unlabeled data to find patterns or groupings.

5. What is reinforcement learning?

   - Answer: A model learns by interacting with an environment and receiving rewards or penalties.

6. What is the difference between AI, ML, and Deep Learning?

- Answer: AI is the broad field, ML is a subset of AI, and Deep Learning is a subset of ML focused on neural networks.

7. What is the bias-variance tradeoff?

   - Answer: Balancing underfitting (high bias) and overfitting (high variance) to minimize total error.

8. What is overfitting?

   - Answer: When a model learns noise in the training data, harming its generalization to new data.

9. How do you prevent overfitting?

   - Answer: Use more data, regularization, cross-validation, or simplify the model.

10. What is underfitting?

    - Answer: When a model is too simple to capture patterns in the data.

Data Preprocessing

1. What is data normalization?

   - Answer: Scaling data to a standard range (e.g., 0 to 1) to improve model performance.

2. What is feature engineering?

   - Answer: Creating new features or transforming existing ones to improve model performance.

3. What is one-hot encoding?

   - Answer: Converting categorical variables into binary vectors.

4. What is the difference between standardization and normalization?

   ◦ Answer: Standardization scales data to have a mean of 0 and a standard deviation of 1, while normalization scales data to a fixed range (e.g., 0 to 1).

5. What is imputation?

   ◦ Answer: Filling missing values in a dataset using techniques like mean, median, or predictive models.

Supervised Learning

16. What is linear regression?

    ◦ Answer: A model that predicts a continuous output by fitting a linear relationship between inputs and outputs.

17. What is logistic regression?

    ◦ Answer: A model used for binary classification by predicting probabilities using a logistic function.

18. What is the difference between regression and classification?

    ◦ Answer: Regression predicts continuous values, while classification predicts discrete labels.

19. What is a decision tree?

    ◦ Answer: A tree-like model that splits data based on feature values to make predictions.

20. What is a random forest?

    ◦ Answer: An ensemble of decision trees trained on random subsets of data to improve accuracy and reduce overfitting.

21. **What is gradient boosting?**

   ○ Answer: An ensemble technique where models are trained sequentially to correct errors of previous models.

22. **What is SVM (Support Vector Machine)?**

   ○ Answer: A model that finds the optimal hyperplane to separate data points of different classes.

23. **What is k-nearest neighbors (KNN)?**

   ○ Answer: A model that predicts the class of a data point based on the majority class of its k-nearest neighbors.

24. **What is Naive Bayes?**

   ○ Answer: A probabilistic model based on Bayes' theorem, assuming independence between features.

25. **What is the difference between bagging and boosting?**

   ○ Answer: Bagging trains models independently and averages predictions, while boosting trains models sequentially to correct errors.

Unsupervised Learning

26. **What is k-means clustering?**

   ○ Answer: An algorithm that partitions data into k clusters by minimizing variance within clusters.

27. **What is hierarchical clustering?**

   ○ Answer: A clustering method that builds a hierarchy of clusters.

28. **What is PCA (Principal Component Analysis)?**

- ◦ Answer: A dimensionality reduction technique that transforms data into a set of orthogonal components.

29. What is t-SNE?

- ◦ Answer: A technique for visualizing high-dimensional data in 2D or 3D.

30. What is the difference between clustering and classification?

- ◦ Answer: Clustering groups unlabeled data, while classification assigns labels to data.

Evaluation Metrics

31. What is accuracy?

- ◦ Answer: The ratio of correct predictions to total predictions.

32. What is precision?

- ◦ Answer: The ratio of true positives to total predicted positives.

33. What is recall?

- ◦ Answer: The ratio of true positives to total actual positives.

34. What is the F1 score?

- ◦ Answer: The harmonic mean of precision and recall.

35. What is a confusion matrix?

- ◦ Answer: A table showing true positives, true negatives, false positives, and false negatives.

36. What is ROC-AUC?

- Answer: A metric that measures the model's ability to distinguish between classes.

37. What is mean squared error (MSE)?

  - Answer: The average squared difference between predicted and actual values.

38. What is R-squared?

  - Answer: A metric that measures the proportion of variance explained by the model.

Deep Learning

39. What is a neural network?

  - Answer: A computational model inspired by the human brain, consisting of layers of interconnected neurons.

40. What is backpropagation?

  - Answer: An algorithm for training neural networks by propagating errors backward and updating weights.

41. What is an activation function?

  - Answer: A function that introduces non-linearity into a neural network (e.g., ReLU, sigmoid).

42. What is dropout?

  - Answer: A regularization technique that randomly drops neurons during training to prevent overfitting.

43. What is a convolutional neural network (CNN)?

- ◦ Answer: A neural network designed for image processing, using convolutional layers.

44. What is a recurrent neural network (RNN)?

    - ◦ Answer: A neural network designed for sequential data, using loops to retain information.

45. What is LSTM?

    - ◦ Answer: A type of RNN that uses memory cells to capture long-term dependencies.

46. What is transfer learning?

    - ◦ Answer: Using a pre-trained model as a starting point for a new task.

Advanced Topics

47. What is the curse of dimensionality?

    - ◦ Answer: As the number of features increases, data becomes sparse, making it harder to model.

48. What is regularization?

    - ◦ Answer: Adding a penalty term to the loss function to prevent overfitting.

49. What is the difference between L1 and L2 regularization?

    - ◦ Answer: L1 adds absolute values of coefficients, while L2 adds squared values.

50. What is gradient descent?

    - ◦ Answer: An optimization algorithm that minimizes the loss function by iteratively adjusting parameters.

51. What is stochastic gradient descent (SGD)?

   ◦ Answer: A variant of gradient descent that uses a single data point at a time.

52. What is batch gradient descent?

   ◦ Answer: A variant of gradient descent that uses the entire dataset at once.

53. What is cross-validation?

   ◦ Answer: A technique for evaluating models by splitting data into multiple subsets.

54. What is hyperparameter tuning?

   ◦ Answer: Optimizing hyperparameters (e.g., learning rate) to improve model performance.

55. What is grid search?

   ◦ Answer: A hyperparameter tuning technique that exhaustively searches a predefined parameter space.

56. What is random search?

   ◦ Answer: A hyperparameter tuning technique that randomly samples from a parameter space.

Practical Questions

57. How do you handle missing data?

   ◦ Answer: Use imputation techniques like mean, median, or predictive models.

58. How do you handle categorical data?

- Answer: Use one-hot encoding or label encoding.

59. How do you deal with imbalanced datasets?

- Answer: Use techniques like oversampling, undersampling, or SMOTE.

60. What is feature selection?

- Answer: Selecting the most relevant features to improve model performance.

61. What is feature extraction?

- Answer: Transforming raw data into a reduced set of features.

62. What is a pipeline in ML?

- Answer: A sequence of data processing steps (e.g., preprocessing, modeling).

63. What is the difference between batch processing and online learning?

- Answer: Batch processing uses the entire dataset, while online learning updates the model incrementally.

64. What is A/B testing?

- Answer: A statistical method to compare two versions of a model or system.

65. What is the difference between parametric and non-parametric models?

- Answer: Parametric models have a fixed number of parameters, while non-parametric models grow with data.

Algorithms

66. What is the difference between gradient boosting and AdaBoost?

   ◦ Answer: Gradient boosting minimizes loss functions, while AdaBoost focuses on misclassified samples.

67. What is XGBoost?

   ◦ Answer: An optimized implementation of gradient boosting.

68. What is LightGBM?

   ◦ Answer: A gradient boosting framework designed for speed and efficiency.

69. What is CatBoost?

   ◦ Answer: A gradient boosting algorithm optimized for categorical data.

70. What is the difference between k-means and DBSCAN?

   ◦ Answer: K-means requires the number of clusters, while DBSCAN does not.

71. What is the difference between PCA and LDA?

   ◦ Answer: PCA maximizes variance, while LDA maximizes class separability.

72. What is the difference between bagging and stacking?

   ◦ Answer: Bagging combines models independently, while stacking uses a meta-model to combine predictions.

73. What is the difference between a generative and discriminative model?

   ◦ Answer: Generative models learn the joint probability distribution, while discriminative models learn the conditional probability.

74. What is the difference between a shallow and deep neural network?

   ◦ Answer: Shallow networks have few layers, while deep networks have many layers.

75. What is the difference between a CNN and an RNN?

   ◦ Answer: CNNs are used for spatial data (e.g., images), while RNNs are used for sequential data (e.g., text).

Miscellaneous

76. What is the difference between machine learning and statistics?

   ◦ Answer: Machine learning focuses on prediction, while statistics focuses on inference.

77. What is the difference between machine learning and data mining?

   ◦ Answer: Machine learning focuses on algorithms, while data mining focuses on discovering patterns in data.

78. What is the difference between a loss function and a cost function?

   ◦ Answer: A loss function measures error for a single data point, while a cost function measures error for the entire dataset.

79. What is the difference between a parameter and a hyperparameter?

   ◦ Answer: Parameters are learned during training, while hyperparameters are set before training.

80. What is the difference between a batch and an epoch?

   ◦ Answer: A batch is a subset of data used in one iteration, while an epoch is one full pass through the dataset.

81. What is the difference between a feature and a target variable?

- ◦ Answer: A feature is an input variable, while a target variable is the output to be predicted.

82. What is the difference between a training set and a test set?

   - ◦ Answer: A training set is used to train the model, while a test set is used to evaluate it.

83. What is the difference between a validation set and a test set?

   - ◦ Answer: A validation set is used for tuning hyperparameters, while a test set is used for final evaluation.

84. What is the difference between a model and an algorithm?

   - ◦ Answer: An algorithm is a procedure, while a model is the output of an algorithm trained on data.

85. What is the difference between a linear and nonlinear model?

   - ◦ Answer: A linear model assumes a linear relationship between inputs and outputs, while a nonlinear model does not.

Case Studies

86. How would you build a recommendation system?

   - ◦ Answer: Use collaborative filtering, content-based filtering, or hybrid methods.

87. How would you detect fraud in transactions?

   - ◦ Answer: Use anomaly detection techniques like isolation forests or autoencoders.

88. How would you classify images?

   - ◦ Answer: Use a convolutional neural network (CNN).

89. How would you predict stock prices?

   ◦ Answer: Use time series models like ARIMA or LSTMs.

90. How would you perform sentiment analysis?

   ◦ Answer: Use NLP techniques like word embeddings and RNNs.

Behavioral Questions

91. Describe a challenging ML project you worked on.

   ◦ Answer: Provide a detailed example, highlighting your approach and results.

92. How do you stay updated with ML trends?

   ◦ Answer: Mention reading research papers, blogs, or attending conferences.

93. What is your favorite ML algorithm, and why?

   ◦ Answer: Choose an algorithm and explain its strengths.

94. How do you handle failure in ML projects?

   ◦ Answer: Discuss learning from mistakes and iterating on solutions.

95. What is your experience with cloud platforms for ML?

   ◦ Answer: Mention experience with AWS, GCP, or Azure.

Coding Questions

96. Write code for linear regression.

   ◦ Answer: Use libraries like Scikit-learn or implement from scratch.

97. Write code for k-means clustering.

   ◦ Answer: Use Scikit-learn or implement from scratch.

98. Write code for a decision tree.

   ◦ Answer: Use Scikit-learn or implement from scratch.

99. Write code for a neural network.

   ◦ Answer: Use TensorFlow or PyTorch.

100. Write code for cross-validation.

   ◦ Answer: Use Scikit-learn's cross_val_score.

Difference Questions with Answers
1. Difference Between Supervised and Unsupervised Learning

- Supervised Learning:

   ◦ Uses labeled data (input-output pairs).
   ◦ Goal is to predict outputs for new inputs.
   ◦ Examples: Classification, Regression.

- Unsupervised Learning:

   ◦ Uses unlabeled data.
   ◦ Goal is to find patterns or groupings in the data.
   ◦ Examples: Clustering, Dimensionality Reduction.

2. Difference Between Classification and Regression

- Classification:

   ◦ Predicts discrete labels (e.g., spam or not spam).
   ◦ Output is a category.

- Regression:

    - Predicts continuous values (e.g., house prices).
    - Output is a number.

3. Difference Between Overfitting and Underfitting

- Overfitting:

    - Model learns noise in the training data.
    - Performs well on training data but poorly on unseen data.

- Underfitting:

    - Model is too simple to capture patterns in the data.
    - Performs poorly on both training and unseen data.

4. Difference Between Bias and Variance

- Bias:

    - Error due to overly simplistic assumptions in the model.
    - Leads to underfitting.

- Variance:

    - Error due to the model's sensitivity to small fluctuations in the training data.
    - Leads to overfitting.

5. Difference Between Bagging and Boosting

- Bagging:

    - Trains multiple models independently on random subsets of data.
    - Combines predictions by averaging (e.g., Random Forest).

- Boosting:

- Trains models sequentially, with each model correcting the errors of the previous one.
- Combines predictions using weighted voting (e.g., AdaBoost, Gradient Boosting).

6. Difference Between L1 and L2 Regularization

- L1 Regularization (Lasso):

  - Adds the absolute value of coefficients to the loss function.
  - Can shrink some coefficients to zero, performing feature selection.

- L2 Regularization (Ridge):

  - Adds the squared value of coefficients to the loss function.
  - Shrinks coefficients but does not set them to zero.

7. Difference Between Precision and Recall

- Precision:

  - Ratio of true positives to total predicted positives (TP / (TP + FP)).
  - Measures accuracy of positive predictions.

- Recall:

  - Ratio of true positives to total actual positives (TP / (TP + FN)).
  - Measures the model's ability to find all positive instances.

8. Difference Between Generative and Discriminative Models

- Generative Models:

  - Learn the joint probability distribution of inputs and outputs.
  - Examples: Naive Bayes, GANs.

- Discriminative Models:

- Learn the conditional probability of outputs given inputs.
- Examples: Logistic Regression, SVM.

9. Difference Between Parametric and Non-Parametric Models

- Parametric Models:

  - Have a fixed number of parameters.
  - Examples: Linear Regression, Logistic Regression.

- Non-Parametric Models:

  - Number of parameters grows with the size of the data.
  - Examples: Decision Trees, k-Nearest Neighbors.

10. Difference Between Batch Gradient Descent and Stochastic Gradient Descent

- Batch Gradient Descent:

  - Uses the entire dataset to compute the gradient in each iteration.
  - Slower but more stable.

- Stochastic Gradient Descent (SGD):

  - Uses a single data point to compute the gradient in each iteration.
  - Faster but noisier.

11. Difference Between k-Means and Hierarchical Clustering

- k-Means:

  - Partitions data into k clusters.
  - Requires the number of clusters (k) to be specified.

- Hierarchical Clustering:

  - Builds a hierarchy of clusters.

- Does not require the number of clusters to be specified.

12. Difference Between PCA and t-SNE

- PCA:

  - Linear dimensionality reduction technique.
  - Focuses on preserving global structure.

- t-SNE:

  - Nonlinear dimensionality reduction technique.
  - Focuses on preserving local structure.

13. Difference Between CNN and RNN

- CNN (Convolutional Neural Network):

  - Used for spatial data (e.g., images).
  - Uses convolutional layers to capture spatial patterns.

- RNN (Recurrent Neural Network):

  - Used for sequential data (e.g., text, time series).
  - Uses loops to retain information over time.

14. Difference Between Gradient Boosting and AdaBoost

- Gradient Boosting:

  - Minimizes loss functions using gradient descent.
  - Builds models sequentially to correct errors.

- AdaBoost:

  - Focuses on misclassified samples by adjusting their weights.
  - Builds models sequentially to improve accuracy.

15. Difference Between Random Forest and Gradient Boosting

- Random Forest:

  - Uses bagging to train multiple decision trees independently.
  - Combines predictions by averaging.

- Gradient Boosting:

  - Uses boosting to train models sequentially.
  - Combines predictions using weighted voting.

16. Difference Between Deep Learning and Machine Learning

- Machine Learning:

  - Includes a broad range of algorithms (e.g., linear regression, decision trees).
  - Often requires feature engineering.

- Deep Learning:

  - Subset of ML focused on neural networks with many layers.
  - Automatically learns features from data.

17. Difference Between Batch Processing and Online Learning

- Batch Processing:

  - Uses the entire dataset to train the model.
  - Suitable for static datasets.

- Online Learning:

  - Updates the model incrementally as new data arrives.
  - Suitable for streaming data.

18. Difference Between Feature Selection and Feature Extraction

- Feature Selection:

  - Selects a subset of existing features.
  - Reduces dimensionality without transforming data.

- Feature Extraction:

  - Creates new features from existing ones.
  - Transforms data into a lower-dimensional space.

19. Difference Between Training Set and Test Set

- Training Set:

  - Used to train the model.
  - Typically 70-80% of the data.

- Test Set:

  - Used to evaluate the model's performance.
  - Typically 20-30% of the data.

20. Difference Between Validation Set and Test Set

- Validation Set:

  - Used to tune hyperparameters and evaluate model performance during training.
  - Helps prevent overfitting.

- Test Set:

  - Used to evaluate the final model's performance after training.
  - Should not be used for tuning.

21. Difference Between Loss Function and Cost Function

- Loss Function:

- Measures error for a single data point.

- Cost Function:

  - Measures error for the entire dataset.

22. Difference Between Epoch and Batch

- Epoch:

  - One full pass through the entire dataset.

- Batch:

  - A subset of the dataset used in one iteration of training.

23. Difference Between k-Nearest Neighbors (kNN) and k-Means

- kNN:

  - Supervised learning algorithm for classification or regression.
  - Predicts based on the k-nearest neighbors.

- k-Means:

  - Unsupervised learning algorithm for clustering.
  - Groups data into k clusters.

24. Difference Between SVM and Logistic Regression

- SVM:

  - Finds the optimal hyperplane to separate classes.
  - Can handle nonlinear boundaries using kernels.

- Logistic Regression:

  - Predicts probabilities using a logistic function.

∘ Limited to linear decision boundaries.

25. Difference Between Deep Learning and Reinforcement Learning

- Deep Learning:

  ∘ Focuses on training neural networks to learn patterns in data.

- Reinforcement Learning:

  ∘ Focuses on training agents to make decisions by interacting with an environment.

These difference-based questions cover a wide range of topics in machine learning. Be prepared to explain these concepts clearly and provide examples where applicable.